THE RIGHT WAY
TO KEEP PET FISH

Where to find *Right Way*

Elliot *Right Way* take pride in our editorial quality, accuracy and value-for-money. Booksellers everywhere can rapidly obtain any *Right Way* book for you. If you have been particularly pleased with any one title, do please mention this to your bookseller as personal recommendation helps us enormously.

Please send to the address on the back of the title page opposite, a stamped, self-addressed envelope if you would like a copy of our *free catalogue*. Alternatively, you may wish to browse through our extensive range of informative titles arranged by subject on the Internet at **www.right-way.co.uk**

We welcome views and suggestions from readers as well as from prospective authors; do please write to us or e-mail: **info@right-way.co.uk**

Reginald Dutta's

THE RIGHT WAY
TO KEEP
PET FISH

Edited and with additional
material by Dick Mills

RIGHT WAY

Typeset in 11pt by Letterpart Limited, Reigate, Surrey.

Printed and bound in Great Britain by Cox & Wyman Ltd., Reading, Berkshire.

The *Right Way* series is published by Elliot Right Way Books, Brighton Road, Lower Kingswood, Tadworth, Surrey, KT20 6TD, U.K. For information about our company and the other books we publish, visit our web site at www.right-way.co.uk

CONTENTS

FOREWORD

When I was originally asked to revise Mr Dutta's longstanding work on aquarium-keeping, it brought me full circle, for way back in 1947 I bought my first aquarium from his Fish Tanks Ltd establishment in London. Since those times, the aquarium hobby has progressed enormously: no longer are glazed tin boxes the norm, and fishes from both coldwater and tropical waters, freshwater and marine are now kept worldwide with the minimum of troubles.

However, the tenets propounded by Reginald Dutta still hold good and anyone keeping fish today would find little to criticise even in his original edition of this work, such was the soundness of his theories. Of course, with the passage of time, we are constantly adding to our knowledge and so it is my pleasurable task to update this book again – to include what is current thinking and outline latest developments, without detracting from the attraction and individualistic style that Reginald Dutta brought to all his written works.

I am especially grateful to the publishers for allowing me to expand the scope of the book to include the care of keeping tropical marine fishes, something that simply was not possible for the average fishkeeper at the time that the original work was written. I am sure that Reginald Dutta would have been just as eager to include information on this now firmly-established, and successful, aspect of fishkeeping to complete his work, had things been different.

Fishkeeping can be a lifelong hobby and this book will not only start you off, but will also keep you, on The Right Way To Keep Pet Fish.

Dick Mills

1

TRUE MEANING OF QUALITY

Why It Is Easy To Cheat A Customer

The trouble with specialised trades, like computers, jewels, or tropical fish, is that it is so very easy to cheat people who have not sufficient knowledge of the subject to protect themselves from unscrupulousness. Methods of 'price clipping' are many and varied, but the following will illustrate the sort of difficulty confronting the customer.

A later chapter describes how to breed good, healthy fish, but there are two important points on which everything depends: firstly, that too many baby fish should not be put in one tank so that they become overcrowded and, through want of sufficient oxygen, food and space, degenerate into poor specimens; secondly, the temperature of the breeding tank should not be kept so high as to cause the fish to grow at an unnatural pace. Under such overcrowding and temperatures the fish become 'forced-bred'. That is to say, when as babies they are kept at higher than normal temperatures, packed into a tank in greater numbers than safety rules allow, often being given strong aeration by pumping air bubbles into their water, then they very quickly grow to saleable size. Such fish can be sold at much lower prices than those reared properly, but they have two very serious disadvantages. They are constitutionally weak and, although not actually sick at the time of sale, are far more liable to disease. They practically never mature into fine specimens in size, shape or colour. Only an expert can detect such frauds – which is what these forced-bred fish are – and almost the sole protection for the public is the reputation of the dealer and their belief in his technical ability.

The dealer is assumed to be a *specialist*. A general knowledge on his part of all forms of pets such as dogs, cats, birds, and so forth is no more satisfactory than is an average knowledge of cookery in judging a cordon bleu chef competition. The aquarist should have a specialised training because his subject is rapidly expanding with many new varieties of fish. The latest research, books, or experts to whom he can turn for information are all so scarce that he cannot hope to give the customer satisfactory service if his energies are dissipated over 'pets' as a whole.

As will be repeatedly shown in this book, the pond or aquarium can be free of trouble *provided* there is specialist knowledge available somewhere along the line; if the customer does not have it, then his dealer simply must fill the gap.

This matter of the customer-dealer relationship is so important that no excuse is made for stressing it. The example given of the forced-bred fish is intended merely as an illustration, and does not exhaust the methods of cutting prices; methods which the customer is unable to prove or even to see. Fortunately, there are a number of ways of helping the customer to form an opinion of the dealer, and the more important are listed below.

Forming An Opinion Of The Dealer

1. Tanks displaying fish for sale should always be of large size.
This is a vital point, the full significance of which is not always understood. In later chapters, the principle of the 'balanced tank', showing how many fish can be kept in it, will be explained, but the point now is that the tanks should be big enough. In a large aquarium the fish may seem few in number, it may appear that the dealer is not offering a good assortment from which to choose; BUT the fish will be healthy – that is what matters.

From the dealer's point of view, the small tank lowers his overhead costs, makes it easier and quicker to catch fish, and gives a better 'display' when lots of fish are jammed together instead of being scattered in large volumes of water. But the customer suffers, as fish kept in such conditions are bound to be weakened and to fall sick unless removed quickly.

2. Fish should be isolated before sale.

Isolation of fish before their sale to the public is a service the good dealer will always give. This is because fish may carry disease, or be sick themselves, so that quarantine of a few days is the only real safeguard. If the fish have been obtained from new or untried sources, for example importations from abroad, a much longer period of separation is required.

The point about isolation is the degree to which it really is carried out; lip-service is one thing, regular and conscientious attention another.

Pressure by the customer who wants 'something cheap' and who compares fish solely/mainly on price has made this service very difficult to maintain, but a few stalwarts still do so. The alternative is to shift the burden on to the (get-it-cheaper) customer and to let him have a quarantine tank of his own for new purchases.

3. General thoroughness.

Apart from the obvious point of having clean tanks, the good dealer will go to the trouble to equalise water temperatures before taking the fish out of one tank to put into another. This point may seem small, but the experienced customer knows its importance, as will be seen by a study of the later chapter on diseases and their causes. There should not be a difference greater than 1°C when fish are being moved from one water to another.

Here, again, there is all the difference between lip-service and not bothering when no customer is looking.

4. Thoughtfulness.

How many catching nets does the dealer use? Beware the person who has only one – so that disease can be transferred from display tank to display tank.

Does the dealer always use the same jar or other container, into which he puts the fish before transferring them to the plastic bag you take home – complete with every disease in the shop?

Does he have warmed wrapping materials handy?

Does he love and know his fish? Or does he scoop up a squirming mass of suffocating/distressed/crushed helpless creatures and then leisurely pick one out by hand? The body temperature for fish is cold; touching it by hand (nearly 38°C) is like taking a red-hot poker to it.

Does he feed his own stock regularly? And with varied foods?

Many are the signs that give away a thoughtless – and, therefore, unsatisfactory – dealer!

Conclusion

The moral of this chapter is that the dealer *must be a specialist* who knows his job, and he must be conscientious and not indulge in price reduction at the expense of quality.

The 'man in the pet shop' did a great service in introducing the hobby to the public, but the march of events has now made his position extremely difficult, as the goldfish-in-a-bowl is as obsolete as the monochrome television. Modern, scientifically balanced aquaria require specialist knowledge constantly kept up to date.

The advantage of patronising the local aquatic dealer cannot be stressed enough. Here you will find someone who is keeping fish in the same water conditions as yours, knows just what species suit these local conditions and will be familiar with the latest technologies.

Regular patronage will ensure that the dealer becomes aware of what fishes interest you, what you have bought in past visits and therefore what species will be compatible with them – even if you don't know yourself. He may even agree to take back unsuitable species or those which have outgrown your aquarium.

In short, always be guided by him; a good dealer won't just be after a quick sale all the time – after all, he wants your regular custom to continue, doesn't he?

2

A COMMUNITY AQUARIUM

In a modern aquarium the water need never be changed completely – never! Before you dismiss this statement as preposterous, please note the word 'completely.' Many newcomers to fishkeeping expect a complete strip-down of the aquarium to be necessary at some time but it is not. Regular partial water changes assist enormously (even if an excellent filtration system is fitted) in maintaining optimum water conditions.

Why The Water Need Never Be Changed

Fish consume oxygen dissolved in water and give off harmful carbon dioxide gases. Basically, all that is necessary is to provide the oxygen supply and get rid of the gases, and this can be done in several ways.

With a sufficiently large surface area, fresh oxygen can be taken in and bad gases escape at a fast enough rate. This is the greatest single factor for success. Relative to the size of the water surface, i.e. the area of water actually in contact with the atmosphere, there should not be too many (or too big) fish otherwise oxygen is consumed and bad gases produced too fast.

Growing plants (under correct lighting conditions), through the process of photosynthesis, break down carbon dioxide and give off excess oxygen during periods of tank illumination (so called 'oxygenators') although plants' natural respiration actually add to carbon dioxide levels – and oxygen consumption – at night.

Water surface turbulence caused by aeration and filtration systems also assist oxygen intake to, and carbon dioxide dispersal from, the aquarium. In theory, the balanced aquarium is thus quite easily obtainable; in practice, correct regular maintenance is equally important. Naturally there should be no excess dirt, especially in the form of uneaten food. The normal usages of regular partial water changes largely discount the objection by purists who maintain that the increase in chemical content over several *years* is detrimental to the fish.

Excess dirt, and excess urine which gives ammonia distress to the fish gill plates, are the chief points of danger to watch for. Your filter (has it been cleaned recently?) should cope with this – if it's big enough! – otherwise you ought to siphon off 30–40% of the water from the tank base and top up with clean warmed water, to replace the tank water thus removed.

Modern power filters are now so good that there should be no problem.

How Deep Should The Tank Be?

It should be noted that the depth of a tank adds little to its fish capacity, as the vital factor is the opening to the air, that is the length and the width from back to front. In fact, excess depth from top to bottom is harmful in that a difference in temperature is caused, since the hotter water rises to the top and the colder water sinks to the bottom. Plants grown in too deep a tank tend to straggle. An irritating number of things seem to 'go wrong' with these deep tanks, the reasons not being always apparent – extra water pressure or failure of light to penetrate down are only partial explanations – but explained or not, deep tanks result in trouble.

This desire for great depth is a common mistake made by the layman, particularly the architect or the interior decorator, and is another illustration why the specialised dealer should be used for guidance; by doing so, a trouble-free aquarium is obtained which will be beautiful and a thing of joy.

If you have a deep tank, then please do have adequate power filtration. Modern techniques of bonding glass to glass are encouraging increased depths, and genuinely strong enough aerators are needed to take the strain.

So long as the water surface is large, there is no harm in using glass covers or close-fitting toplights; even if these were almost airtight there would be enough oxygen in a cushion of air 1 or 2cm thick, trapped between the top of the water and the glass cover, to last a good many hours; nor should the carbon dioxide concentration become harmful in that period. During this time the cover should normally be displaced, even momentarily, for feeding, etc., thus renewing the oxygen supply of this air cushion and letting out the used-up 'bad' air.

How Many Fish In A Tank?
The following are guiding principles for the number of fish in a community tank; but in case of doubt a specialist should be consulted. Air-operated filters increase this capacity by 40%, power filters by 100%.

Number of tropical fish, average body length 3cm	Area of tank water surface	Suggested depth of tank, top to bottom
18	45cm x 30cm	30cm – 38cm
24–28	60cm x 30cm	30cm – 45cm
36–40	90cm x 30cm	30cm –50cm
48–55	120cm x 30cm	30cm – 60cm

Coldwater Fish
Usually these are much larger than tropicals and one body centimetre of fish, measured lengthways, is calculated to consume the oxygen absorbed by 365 square centimetres of water surface (same as the number of days in the year). Hence very few, and very small, coldwater fish can be kept in an aquarium; Goldfish, Rudd, Orfe, Carp, etc., are *not* suitable and they are better in outdoor ponds. The cruelty of keeping Goldfish in a bowl is clear: the air surface of the bowl is too small to supply oxygen for a fast-moving, quick-growing type like a Goldfish, even if it lingers on in its uncomfortably cramped prison for a few years, stunted in growth and suffer-

ing in slow suffocation. A Goldfish should normally live a quarter of a century in the more natural environment of a pond, but even then for your garden pond we suggest slow-moving (less oxygen consuming) fish that do not grow too fast, for example Shubunkins, Fantails, Telescopic-eyed Moors, Veiltails, Lionheads, Orandas, but *not* Goldfish!

The above are safe capacity guides, allowing for such factors as increased heat causing the water to have a lower oxygen content, or for excess dirt causing a limited amount of fouling. The suggested number of fish can be exceeded, particularly by the addition of aeration, and if you do have more fish, it is recommended. So beware of buying new fish from tanks crowded beyond these limits, or of overcrowding your own.

Dangers

Shells, ornaments and rocks can most certainly be used in a community aquarium, but only with great care as a danger-ously high proportion are harmful to fish.

Many kinds of rock, in particular, slowly dissolve in water, resulting in an imperceptible but definite clouding of the water, and much more important, this dissolution alters the chemical content of the water with results that are harmful to fish even to the point of death. Yet rocks add greatly to the beauty of the aquascape. Several guaranteed harmless types are now sold and their use is enjoyed by thousands of aquarists. Your dealer must guide you in this matter.

An important point to remember is that within reason it is not the volume of water which counts but the area in contact with the air. Thus if a tank is lavishly decorated with gravel and aquatic rocks, giving a beautiful effect but displacing some of the water, there is no harm done because the air surface has not been reduced. Piling the gravel in hills and dales so that the fish have varying depths of water to choose from is helpful to their health, in addition to being decorative.

Technical knowledge is also vital in the case of the substrate material used at the bottom of the aquarium. If too fine it will seem to 'matt' down and choke the plants' roots; if too coarse it tends to trap greater amounts of food and excreta and so causes fouling. It is also true that fish like to pick up mouthfuls of substrate material, 'chewing it over' and keeping the nourishing particles mixed therein, spitting out the rest. Thus substrate material composition must be suitable for this purpose.

Plants And Light

Soil, loam, etc., are unnecessary for the ordinary growth of plants in a community aquarium; it is another matter when propagating plants on a commercial scale or growing extra fine specimens where the fish are a secondary consideration.

Light is necessary for the health of the plants to enable them to absorb the carbon dioxide gases the fish breathe out. Too much light will cause the appearance of microscopic life known as algae, and cause the water to turn green; insufficient light kills the plants.

In general, the aquarium in a bright room should have about 4 hours' artificial light; in a dark room up to 12 or even 14 hours daily. The strength of the artificial light should be approximately 25 watts per 900cm^2 of water surface, and an electric bulb should be within 10cm of the water. For general illumination, fluorescent tubes are more often used; tubes with different light spectra can be fitted for colour enhancement, extra plant growth or even to simulate moonlight, according to the fishkeeper's tastes and the aquarium's needs. Two advantages of fluorescent lighting are that the tubes do not give out as much heat as 'bulbs' and also consume less electricity – 10 watts per 30cm length of aquarium is a good starting guide.

Concentration of light in one spot, leaving the rest of the tank in semi-darkness, ruins the oxygenating plants and causes all sorts of trouble. Many aquariums are now sold as complete fully-fitted items, having fluorescent lighting already installed: although quite adequate for general fish viewing, sometimes it will be necessary to add another tube (and starting gear) for satisfactory plant growth.

An aquarium is better situated in a dark spot where the amount of light it receives can be exactly controlled by using electric bulbs, instead of relying on the whims of daylight. By contrast, too, the internal aquarium lighting shows up better in a dark corner.

The 'Gro-lux' type of lighting that eliminates the 'yellow cast' in water and which highlights the colours of the fish, especially the blues, reds and greens, has become deservedly popular.

Many people also like 'speciality lighting'. Secondary illumination, perhaps shining 'from afar' or through the water (as distinct from above), gives a soft, muted effect, soothing and relaxing to the onlooker.

Of course, with today's disco lighting technology it would be quite possible to 'programme' the aquarium's lighting pattern. Indeed, units are available which slowly build up light in the morning to a blaze of brightness at noon followed by a tranquil fading down at dusk. (Time switches will maintain lighting periods during occasions of absence.) However, any *sudden* changes in lighting levels will stress or startle the fish; at night, make a practice of switching off the aquarium *before* the room lights; in the morning, switch on the *room lights* before those over the aquarium.

A Cautionary Word

With both glass and glass-bonding adhesives being readily available, the temptation to 'make your own aquarium' seems a very feasible prospect, especially if the tank size you want isn't available as an 'off the shelf' item from your dealer. However, therein lie several dangers.

Obviously any glass chosen must give a distortion-free view of the aquarium, but the *thickness* of glass used must be chosen according to the size of the tank to allow for the not inconsiderable water pressure imposed upon it: tanks up to 600mm in length by 450mm deep require 6mm thick glass, increasing by 2mm in thickness for every extra 300mm in length or 100mm in water depth. Most commercially available tanks now display a trade body's sticker showing that the thickness of the glass fitted conforms to a safe standard.

Not all sealants are suitable and it is vital that only those formulated especially for aquarium applications are used – many apparently suitable sealants, such as bathroom and kitchen types found in DIY outlets, contain fish-harming anti-mould and anti-fungus additives.

In the face of such factors, surely it is better all round to buy a properly made aquarium rather than try to save a few pounds and put both your family's and your fishes' safety at risk.

Conclusion

If the above points seem complicated, it should be remembered that a specialised dealer would take care of them automatically, and the customer's co-operation would be limited in practice to switching the electric light on for the required number of hours. If no specialised knowledge is available, trouble is encountered unnecessarily. These remarks apply to all aquaria, whether coldwater or tropical.

3

SETTING UP THE TANK

The first thing to decide is its situation. A place where the aquarium is subject to wide fluctuations in room temperature is not the best – for example, right by an outside window where the outside air might change from hot to cold, throwing unnecessary strain on the internal heating elements of the tank; in this case the back of the aquarium should be separated from the window glass by some form of insulation, such as a sheet of cardboard, plywood, felt, etc. Excess light from the window can turn the water green, as explained in Chapter 2, unless shading is provided.

Instructions on installing the freshwater aquarium are usually supplied at the time of sale, but the following, listed in order of operation, may prove of interest. Stages 2 and 7 may be disregarded for coldwater aquariums. Stage 8 is for marine aquariums only.

1. The substrate material to be used, usually fine gravel, should be thoroughly washed. This must be done most painstakingly, as dirt left in it will later cloud the tank. It is easier to wash gravel in small doses. The inside of the aquarium could be cleaned first and the newly washed gravel then introduced bit by bit as it is ready; otherwise water from the washed gravel would seep all over the place. Don't forget to install the undergravel filter system first!

Incidentally, never try moving aquariums when full – they are far too heavy! However, when setting up, the substrate can be placed in small aquariums (up to 45cm long) wherever is convenient and the partially furnished tank then set in its final chosen site. As all-glass aquariums have no supporting 'frame' it is not uncommon to find glass bracing straps, from front to back, across the top of large tanks; another warning, don't try to lift the aquarium by these, nor by the glass ledges (on which the hood sits) around the top of the tank. All-glass tanks should 'sit' on a thick sheet of expanded polystyrene to cushion them against uneven surfaces.

2.   In the case of the tropical tank, a heater and thermostat (usually a combined unit these days) should be fitted. There are many types of these available but none is difficult to fit.

3.   The gravel and the guaranteed harmless rocks should be arranged to suit your artistic taste, but the heater should be kept right down at the lowest point of the tank since heat rises; if the gravel is arranged in hills and dales, the heater ought to be positioned horizontally in a dale. Care should be taken, however, to mount the unit clear of the substrate to ensure adequate water circulation around it.

Heaped-up gravel should be anchored by rocks, otherwise it will flatten out when water is poured in. Sometimes the substrate is arranged to slope down to the front; in this way sediment and droppings from the fish tend to accumulate there and are more easily siphoned off, as explained below.

4.   The tank should be filled gently, very gently. The freshwater aquarium is filled using ordinary tap water to which a dechlorinating agent is added; this additive (available from your aquatic dealer) also neutralizes any heavy metals in the water and makes it more immediately suitable for aquarium use. If you are intending to keep fish which require special water conditions different from those of your tap water, then the water should be treated, or made up, accordingly.

A plate held at substrate level will break the fall of the water and will therefore prevent the substrate churning up and clouding the tank – often for days. Once the tank has been filled it should not be moved, otherwise the internal pressure will cause leaks.

5.   A sufficient number of plants should be planted to create a balanced tank; usually it is preferred to group in bunches, but these should not be too thick or inserted too deeply into the substrate. In the case of large tanks, planting can be done when only half full of water. The plants with roots should have covering only as far as their 'crown' – that is, so that the white part is buried but not the green; cuttings should be inserted up to 1.5cm. *It is important that all plants be kept wet while these operations are being carried out*, otherwise later they will tend to shrivel in the aquarium – sometimes very quickly – or at the least their growth will be seriously retarded. A judicious combination of plant thickets and 'caves' formed by rocks will provide hiding places for fish if they are off-colour.

6.   The toplight, usually supplied with the aquarium, should be connected and plugged in.

7.   To adjust the thermostat, three things should be remembered:

(a) The water takes a long time to change temperature (from one to four hours), so an adjustment of the control knob of the thermostat does not show an altered reading on the thermometer for some time.

(b) *Very slight* adjustments of the control knob of the thermostat are all that are required, perhaps an eighth, a quarter, or at most half a turn will suffice.

(c) Once the thermostat has been set at the required temperature, further adjustments should be unnecessary, as this temperature will be automatically maintained.

8.   With the marine aquarium, synthetic seawater must be prepared ahead of setting up the aquarium and checked for the correct Specific Gravity (SG) using an aquarium hydrometer.

Check the SG value at the operating temperature of the aquarium. It should read between 1.020 – 1.024 although dealers often keep it lower to save salt and control parasites.

All is now ready. In all cases, it is advisable to wait five days, or even a week, to allow the plants to grow, the undergravel filter (if fitted) to mature and the water to get 'old' before introducing the fish. Water that has been standing for some time under the action of light becomes 'old', that is, develops microscopic life – a fact greatly appreciated by the fish.

PLANTS

Plants are often classified as tropical and coldwater, but it is proposed here to divide them into aquarium or pond plants because hot-house-grown (or tropical) plants will root in a coldwater tank kept in the normal living room of a home, especially if an aquarium toplight is functioning. Strictly coldwater plants, on the other hand, are normally considered to be those that will thrive out in the open, winter or summer.

There is an important amount of interchange between the two categories, but the main distinction remains: those grown with the aid of artificial heat, e.g. in a hot house, are for an aquarium, and those grown in the open are for a pond. It should be noted that although the same plant is often found both indoors and out, the pond one tends to be larger and coarser and not exactly the same as the one in the aquarium.

The Need For Plants

Plants are not merely decorative and pleasing in appearance but are essential to complete the scientific balance of the modern aquarium. This has been dealt with in Chapter 2 and need not be enlarged upon.

Further, the majority of community fish have a definite preference for a planted tank where they can find shade, privacy and hiding places when they are feeling out of sorts or are anxious to evade the attentions of a particular fish, be it a bully, a rival, or too ardent a suitor.

Plants can also play a major role during fish breeding. Many species will find that the firm, flat leaves of some plants make

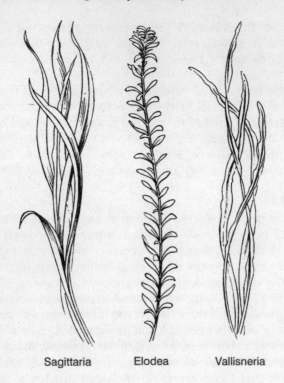

Sagittaria   Elodea   Vallisneria

Fig. 1

ideal spawning sites; bushy plants will make excellent spawning receptacles, catching the falling fertilised eggs and effectively shielding them from the hungry, post-spawning adult fish. Floating plants are often incorporated in the bubble nest of spawning Anabantoid fishes, whilst the resultant young fish from any spawning will find refuge amongst bushy plants or the long trailing 'roots' of floating plants.

Care Of Aquarium Plants

As previously mentioned, plants in a community tank need light. They should be rooted in aquarium gravel, but not too deeply, and loam, earth, etc., are not necessary for their growth. Loam can breed harmful bacteria unless sterilised, and if this is done then the loam is of little use to the plants; after all, part of the plants' function in a balanced tank is to 'absorb' the droppings of the fish – these fertilising media being broken up by the plants – simultaneously promoting their own growth and materially helping to dispose of the droppings.

Propagation is done in two ways. *Vallisneria* and similar plants send out runners which develop into new roots that can be broken off and grown separately; *Myriophyllum* and *Ludwigia* and such others have cuttings taken from them at the nodes, and these will root of their own accord when planted.

Lead weights wrapped around the base are sometimes used to prevent the newly transferred plants from floating to the surface of the water, but they are very liable to damage the plants unless used most carefully; in any case, a little patience and a substrate depth of 3cm should make weights quite unnecessary. If planting pots or trays are favoured, they should be big enough and deep enough to allow for root growth, say 5cm deep and 5cm wide.

A final reminder about these lovely aquatic plants is to keep them wet; if they are allowed to dry even momentarily, for example when being transferred or while in the process of being planted, they will suffer for weeks; in fact, they will sometimes shrivel and die. Also, great care must be taken if, for any reason, the aquarium is being disinfected. The plants can easily be damaged by being rinsed in water that is too hot or in a disinfectant that is too strong. One quarter grain by weight of potassium permanganate in 4.5 litres of water makes a strong enough solution to wash off most parasites from the leaves.

Planting effects are more decorative if done in thickets and not in single stems. Obviously, the thickets should not be congested so that the individual stems do not have enough room to grow; four to eight in a bunch is reasonable. Provided that the fish can swim about freely, there is little danger of the aquarium being overcrowded. The disadvantage of plants taking in oxygen at night, instead of giving it out, is not serious if the aquarium has a large enough air surface, as emphasised in Chapter 2.

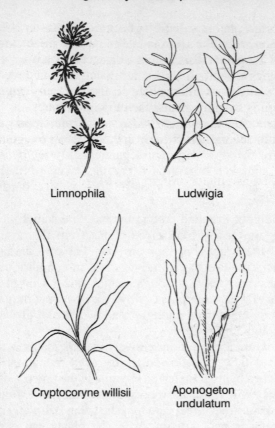

Limnophila   Ludwigia

Cryptocoryne willisii   Aponogeton undulatum

Fig. 2

It helps if the aquarium light is kept on for longer periods when the greenery is first planted so as to give the plants a better chance to take root; this is particularly true in winter when natural growth is slow.

It is not proposed to describe the individual specimens in great detail, nor their various subdivisions, but the following general description of the more common plants may be of interest.

Strong Oxygenators

These are plants that give off more oxygen than most. *Vallisneria* and *Sagittaria* are two of the best; from the illustrations it will be seen that they are very similar, *Sagittaria* being the larger and coarser. *Vallisneria* leaves have a stripe down the centre, dividing them into three nearly equal stripes of two shades of green. Both plants are normally found in three types: straight, twisted, and giant; there is also a *Dwarf Sagittaria*. Propagation is by runners that develop into roots.

Anacharis, now known as *Elodea*, propagated from cuttings and found in several varieties, is another strong oxygenator.

Others
All classified hereunder are propagated from cuttings, and are great favourites.

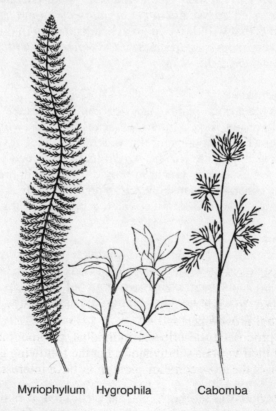

Myriophyllum   Hygrophila   Cabomba

Fig. 3

Ludwigia, some species of which have leaves that are tinged with red; *Hygrophila* is similar, with pointed pale green leaves and woody stems, removing the growing tip results in a bushier plant.

There are other bushy plants, such as *Myriophyllum*, *Ambulia* and *Cabomba*.

Specials
Under this heading comes the tiny, delicate, lovely and hard-to-obtain Hair Grass, *Eleocharis acicularis*.

Also there are plants that form a clump on their own, such as the broad leaved, light green Amazon Sword (*Echinodorus* sp), the serrated edged *Aponogeton undulatum*; and the very useful plants that will thrive in great heat and even in dim light – the *Cryptocorynes*, particularly *Cryptocoryne willisii* and *Cryptocoryne becketti*.

Floating Plants
Numerous aquarium plants just float on the surface of the water and are not rooted in any other medium, drawing their nourishment from the air and the water. The chief favourites among these plants are *Riccia*, *Azolla* and Duckweed (*Lemna* sp). They are especially useful in providing shade in breeding, and as oxygenators because they trap air bubbles from which the oxygen is absorbed into the water, especially at night.

Conclusion
This list makes no attempt to be complete or to go into the various species of each plant, nor does it differentiate between those having roots and those grown from bulbs; neither does it include quite well-known ones that are difficult to obtain, e.g. *Nuphar* Lilies, Madagascar Lace Plant (*Aponogeton fenestralis*), *Acorus*, *Nitella* and many others. Pond plants are described in the chapter on ponds.

Why Do Plants Die?
1. Their roots are too hot if the tank is above a radiator; a protective heat shield over the radiator should normally suffice.

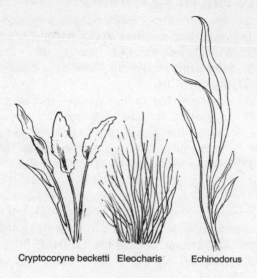

Cryptocoryne becketti Eleocharis   Echinodorus

Fig. 4

2. Too little, or unevenly spaced toplighting, especially if the tank is more than 50cm deep.
3. Water is too acid. See pH details on page 52.
4. Lack of nutrients.
5. Not enough room to grow; e.g. thickets too thick, or lead weights too tight.
6. Wrong kind of plants, or, more rarely, unsuitable water in the tank for that particular type of plant.
7. White flecks on the plants, especially in the morning, mean too few fishes and plants in the tank.
8. Black patches round the plant roots mean too many harmful nitrates; tank needs a good clean up, and better balance.

Plant Fertilisers
Available in liquid and tablet form. All manner of vitalisers are on sale, for example, to help the newly transplanted cuttings or roots; especially useful in winter when growth is normally slow.

AERATION AND FILTRATION

The old air pumps were noisy and unsatisfactory, and were not recommended in earlier writings as it certainly is possible to balance a tank without them. However, the position has radically changed and really fine pumps are now widely available and in general use.

The vibrator pumps, the piston pumps, the magnetic coil pumps, and the water circulating pumps are found everywhere. The stronger the pump, the better the aeration, the greater the flow of returning water, the wider the area it sweeps and the fewer the backwaters left to fester.

Filtration

A filter is a device for removing floating particles of the larger kind from aquarium water and even for adsorbing some of the gases therein. A filter unit, containing a suitable filter medium, may be (depending on design) fitted inside or outside of the aquarium.

The simplest internal and external 'box' filters are operated by an airflow (generated by the airpump) which returns cleaned water to the aquarium after passing through the filter. These days, even the smallest internal or external filter is likely to be powered by a small electrically-driven impeller; these filters have a greater throughput of water than air-driven types and soon repay their initial cost in happy fish and labour-saving of tank clean ups. The impellers are often used separately (when they're known as 'powerheads') to pull water through sub-gravel filtration systems.

The filter normally consists of three layers: the first, such as filter floss, is to remove floating particles; the second, activated carbon, is the core of the apparatus which even removes the gases and some of the organic compounds such as toxic products due to the presence of fish in the water; the third is merely a few layers of ceramic pieces to provide colonisation sites for nitrifying bacteria.

Thus a filter is no more than a container equipped with an airlift, or an impeller, and these three layers. It can be hung inside or outside the aquarium, depending on its size; the amount of work it can do is governed by its own area and by the rate of the water filtering through it. The three layers must, of course, be packed down just tightly enough so that the water has to percolate through and not run down quickly.

The first layer of the filter shows the dirt and indicates the need for change, bearing as it does the brunt of the work by removing the larger floating particles. Most filters and connecting hoses are made from semi-opaque material to discourage the formation of clogging algae.

What Will The Filter Do?
The conventional filter, as previously described, will *mechanically* and *chemically* remove suspended and dissolved matter respectively, equalise water temperature and provide a form of aeration by circulating the water.

It will *not* remove algae or disease-carrying parasites unless a special filter medium is used. Green water, however, can be removed by using an ultra-violet lamp in conjunction with a filter and this process is described later, as it is more pertinent to ponds.

Therefore, is it worth the trouble and expense? Frankly, yes. Like aeration, it is a useful adjunct.

Sub-gravel Filters
These draw oxygenated water through the substrate where colonising bacteria *biologically* break down toxic ammonia-based compounds, changing them into progressively less harmful nitrite and nitrate. These filters may be air-operated or employ a powerhead to move water through the system. Powerhead operation is recommended for use in marine aquariums where a greater turnover of water is required.

One criticism of sub-gravel filters is that, as well as acting biologically, they also act *mechanically* and any dirt drawn into the gravel by the water flow tends to stay there, clogging up the gravel, restricting the water flow and consequently the filter's efficiency. Periodic use of a 'gravel washer' will reduce clogging up to some extent. A better idea is to use the 'reverse-flow' method of operation.

Reverse-flow sub-gravel filters have pre-cleaned water (courtesy of an external power filter) pumped *down* the normal uplift tube so that it circulates back into the main aquarium *upwards* through the gravel; this reversal of water flow also stops sediment settling on the substrate surface too, thus aiding the filter's ability to clear the water. Incidentally, the nitrifying bacteria don't care which way the water flows, just as long as it continues to do so.

Not all biological filters need be 'undergravel' types. 'Fluidised bed' filters are external canisters in which water is constantly pumped through a special sand, held in semi-suspension, on which nitrifying bacteria develop.

In 'trickle filters', with deliberately designed unoxygenated areas, different bacteria change the nitrate further into nitrogen gas.

Conclusion

Do not be tempted to use small (cheap!) filters – you will spend too much time cleaning them out! Regularly clean filter media otherwise toxins may well be washed back into the aquarium. Always wash filter media in aquarium water; using raw tap water will kill off any beneficial nitrifying bacteria present and the filter will lose efficiency until these bacteria re-colonise the washed filter media.

4

GENERAL MAINTENANCE: COLDWATER OR TROPICAL

General Maintenance

The general maintenance of an aquarium is virtually nil. The two golden rules are not to overfeed and not to overcrowd. From time to time, the tank water will evaporate and should be replaced gently with water of the *same temperature*, simply because a waterline that shows spoils the decorative effect. Once a week, or a fortnight, the inside of the aquarium glass can be wiped slowly, to clean it. Either a small scraper bought for the purpose will do, or a piece of lint-free cloth – the smallest and cleanest duster will prove too large and will almost certainly leave annoying pieces of fluff in the water.

If an oily film appears on the water surface, it should be skimmed off. This can be done by placing a sheet of paper flat on the top of the water and drawing it from one side to the other; the oil or grease will cling to the paper and so be removed.

Siphoning

With proper care and no overfeeding, there should be negligible amounts of sediment to remove, and this should be done, say, once a month. Many 'automatic' types of siphon are available and are probably better suited to the average hobbyist. Some, however, prefer to use a bucket and a siphon tube – that is, a piece of rubber tubing about 2 metres long with an approximate diameter of 1cm. By filling this tube with water, from the tap, sealing both ends with the thumbs, and releasing both ends simultaneously (with the aquarium end of the tube under water), the water from the aquarium will flow down into a bucket placed on the floor, and as it flows it will carry the dirt with it. Care should be taken not to siphon out a fish by mistake – something that can happen much more easily than is imagined – and it helps to hold the aquarium end of the siphon tube not more than a fraction above the gravel (and sediment) level. No harm is done if some gravel is siphoned off too. Usually about the bottom 30% of water is removed in this process. The aim is to remove as much sediment and as little water as possible.

When the work is finished, the aquarium should be topped up with water of the *same* temperature.

Introducing New Fish
When a few new fish are being introduced, it is a good plan to feed those already established in the tank extra well, on this one occasion only, and, while they are busy eating at one end, gently to tip in the newcomers at the other end. The new arrivals are thus given a chance to settle down, to find hiding places, and generally to take stock of the situation before meeting the crowd, as it were.

Of course, the water temperatures will have been equalised before the transfer; to do this, the bag containing the fish can be hung, or floated, in the aquarium until its water temperature becomes the same as that of the tank, usually in 15–30 minutes. Once the temperatures have been equalised, the bag may be gently tipped, allowing its water to flow out and the fish to swim straight into the aquarium without being netted or handled.

Bully Fish
Fish that are too boisterous and are inclined to throw their weight about can be 'stood in the corner' by being imprisoned in a large jam jar. The water for the jar must be taken from the aquarium to ensure that there is no temperature change. If the jar is only two thirds full it will float safely in the aquarium and maintain its temperature. The top should be covered lest the fish gets frightened and tries to jump out; it could be

released after 12–24 hours. No smell in the jar, please, of jam, pickles, tobacco, etc.

Catching Fish

Rather than chase the elusive creature all round the tank and ruin the plants and general appearance in the process, it is easier to chase the fish *into* the net.

Holding the net in a good position so that it can quickly be pulled upwards, not forward (because the fish will prove too quick for that), a ruler or another small net can be used to drive the fish into the main net.

Temperature

The temperature range of most aquaria of tropical fish is fairly wide, 18–29°C, with extreme ranges down to 7°C and up to 35°C; but a community tank should normally be kept *between* 22°C and 27°C. Lest the above remark regarding the extreme temperature range be misunderstood, tropical fish in water colder than 20°C will soon die unless heated up within a few hours, but they can perfectly well undertake a 12–18 hour journey by land, sea or air, entailing a marked temperature drop. Provided the water cools *gradually*, fish do not often suffer harm. This factor makes a journey possible, and electricity failures or power cuts not nearly so frightening as some people think.

If emergency measures are needed to keep the fishwater warm, a good plan is to fill a bottle with hot water and immerse this in the aquarium; it is thus possible to retain sufficient heat all night, especially if a covering rug over the whole aquarium is used as well. The introduction of hot water straight into the tank is not advisable as there is a danger of cracking the aquarium glass.

Signs Of Trouble

The hobbyist will soon sense if anything is going wrong with the tank. The first sign of the fish being unwell is that the dorsal fin folds up; this fin on top of the back should be erect. Another sign is when fish go off their food, or keep unusually still, for example at the same corner of the tank – be it at the top or bottom. In such cases pages 39–44 should be consulted, and, if these do not provide sufficient guidance, the help of the specialist dealer should be enlisted as soon as possible.

He will need to be told as much relevant 'case history' as is practicable – whether there are any particular symptoms, any recent purchases, any points of the above-mentioned pages that are applicable. He may require to be shown samples of the aquarium gravel and water. Any dead fish, *freshly* preserved in water or pure alcohol, should also be taken to him for examination.

All this applies to both tropical and to coldwater aquaria.

FEEDING
There are two main foods – live and prepared.

The live are better, but they are difficult to obtain in constant, all-the-year-round supply. Fish will thrive quite well on a mixture of live and prepared foods; in fact, they can get along without *any* live food if that proves necessary.

Amount
The golden rule about feeding is simple: *do not overfeed*. All food given, *including* that which falls to the bottom of the pond or aquarium, should be completely eaten in about three minutes. For example, twelve tropical fish of ordinary size (body measurement about 3cm long) or three coldwater aquaria fish of, say, 5cm body measurement, should be given enough prepared food only to cover this circle:

That is, about a quarter of one pinch – and that is enough. The frequency of feeding is a matter of some controversy, but once or twice a day should be sufficient. Tropical fish at 21°C or below are sluggish and eat little; at 24°C they are ravenous;

at 28°C and above, the lowered oxygen content of the water again robs them of their appetite. Similarly with coldwater fish at, say, 10°C, 18°C and 22°C; the only point is that coldwater fish vary so much in their temperature tolerance that these figures are very, very approximate.

The ideal temperatures are, then: for tropical fish 23°C to 26°C; and for non-tropical 16°C to 19°C.

As is now well known, fish can go long periods without any food whatsoever, so that if the owner plans to be away for a week he need make no special provision for the long-established community tank; the microscopic life already present in the water will be sufficient for that period of time. This course is strongly recommended in preference to allowing an unskilled stranger to feed the fish; a stranger might be tempted to be mistakenly generous with unfortunate results – after all, one pinch a day is four times too much, and spread over a week could dirty a tank. If a stranger *must* be trusted with the feeding, a good idea is to make up tiny packets for him, each sufficient for one day's meal, which he will use and not have to rely on his own judgment. Alternatively, the owner could profitably feed up the fish on live food for ten days or so prior to departure so as to store up surplus fat energy in the fish, on which they can draw in his absence. **But** all traces of excess excreta or uneaten food must be siphoned off before departure lest the water be fouled.

Special 'vacation' blocks that dissolve slowly in water to release predetermined amounts of food are available; the fish can eat this food over a period of days whilst you are away. One such type, for ponds, even releases a visible float when renewal is due!

Types Of Prepared Foods

The choice is almost limitless; every country seems to market its own brands and there is no excuse for a monotonous diet – fish need variety as much as we do.

The old granular, or crumb, type foods have largely been displaced by flakes, manufactured under strict laboratory conditions. Sometimes these offer single ingredients (shrimp, meal, liver, beef, etc.), sometimes they are mixed with vita-

mins, sometimes they are in the form of multi-flake conglom-
erates, and sometimes you find them packed in 'menu' form
where each tin of food has different compartments so that
particular ingredients can be varied at will.

The 'freeze-dried' revolution has added a new dimension:
just as we can get frozen fruits out of season, so too can fish
now get vitamin-fresh freeze-dried delicacies.

Frozen foods also provide the means of obtaining the
nutritional benefits of 'live' foods without the risks of disease
from wild-caught stocks; as a further safeguard, many prepared foods are also irradiated with gamma rays to minimise
the introduction of disease.

Please do not forget that many fish are vegetarians by
preference and rather resent lumps of meat compounds being
flung at them; the answer is to make sure they have adequate
'green stuff' mixture foods, of which plenty are available.

If, in desperation, fish are reduced to eating the tank plants,
do not blame them. It's your fault. Is the diet too monotonous?
Too lop-sided? How many different brands? How much live
food (see below)?

Live Foods
The very best foods are live insects and worms, and these can
usually be obtained from a specialist dealer.

Daphnia is the favourite, universally acknowledged as such.
Red *Tubifex* worms, white *Enchytraea* worms, brine shrimp,
bloodworms and earthworms are also beneficial. The trouble
with gathering these foods from rivers, duckponds and other
natural sources is the very real danger of introducing waterborne enemies and diseases, described in later chapters, and
the hobbyist should be extremely wary on these points; expert
screening is essential before use. Special foods for breeding
are also dealt with later.

Should live foods not be available, a satisfactory substitute
is to hang into the tank, on a cotton thread, a tiny piece of meat
(preferably white), fish, liver, shrimp, prawn, roe, lettuce,
boiled spinach, etc. – in fact almost anything edible that does
not dissolve in water; for example, corned beef contains a high
percentage of fat, which will dirty the water and should not

therefore be used. The substitute can be cooked or raw, but thoroughly washed so as to avoid fouling the water; for instance, the blood from raw meat should have been washed out first. One morsel 3cm long by 3cm thick ought to suffice for twelve standard fish (body measurement 3cm) and should be left in the tank for 30–40 minutes at a time. Again, frequency of feeding is a matter of controversy, but once or twice a day should be ample. If possible, a new substitute should be used each time. Two or three pieces could be hung, at different heights, so as to allow the shy and the weak to feed more easily.

Footnotes
Different kinds of food produce different results. An exclusive diet of oatmeal and of chopped-up white worms is fattening and is sometimes used, as in the case of Veiltail Goldfish, to produce fish with short, rounded bodies, heavy and even a little clumsy. On the other hand, dry prepared foods of the flake type, and the slightly laxative live *Daphnia*, tend to produce normal fast-swimming fish.

Red *Tubifex* worms will stay alive for days in a jam jar, standing under a slow-running tap; the *continuous* flow of water washes away any dead worms leaving the nice bright-red ones in a tight cluster at the bottom of the jar.

Live *Daphnia* are usually sold in plastic bags, containing water and pure oxygen and food for the *Daphnia*, so that these stay alive and fresh for several days – you can now buy a week's supply at only one trip to the shop.

THINGS THAT GO WRONG
All living creatures, whether human or fish, can fall sick. Curing them requires knowledge which the layman cannot hope to acquire without years of study and experience – in other words, without becoming a specialist himself. Therefore he should rely, and rightly so, on his dealer.

As with human diseases, the doctor is called only for the more serious cases, and there are many things the layman can learn so as to be able to recognise signs of danger and to apply the more simple remedies.

Cloudy Water

The first and most obvious sign of trouble is the water becoming cloudy. The cloudiness may be one of three colours: white, brown or green (sometimes turning to yellow).

White cloudiness in the aquarium water is dangerous; it often means that for some reason the oxygen content of the water is too low and the carbon dioxide content is too high. Perhaps there are too many (or too big) fish that are taking the oxygen out of the water quicker than the air is replacing it; it may be a dead fish, snail, mussel, or other decomposing matter that is fouling the tank; it may be something dissolving in the water, for example, a harmful rock, shell or ornament; or it may be that the temperature of the water has risen, automatically reducing the water oxygen content and causing overcrowding and white cloudiness. In any event, white cloudiness has to be tackled at once or the fish will die; it is therefore essential to find the cause, calling in the specialist if necessary, and to change a third of the water at a time, replacing with fresh water of the *same temperature*. The water is changed with an ordinary clean jug or it can be siphoned, whichever is easier.

One complication arises in that green water, dealt with below, appears white in its initial stages, but if the fish show signs of distress it is safe to assume that the clouding of the water is, in fact, white, and to take the foregoing precautions. Obvious distress signals are detailed under heading 14, pages 43-44.

Brown cloudiness is nearly always caused by dirt or by excess food that has not been eaten and lies around the tank, often turning the substrate black: substrate not properly washed, too much sediment at the bottom which should be siphoned off, decaying leaves of plants, or some such cause. Lack of sufficient growing plants is also a contributory cause. Brown cloudiness is unsightly but not particularly dangerous in the first instance, although prolongation of this condition can encourage disease.

Green cloudiness is healthy. Under the action of excess light (sunlight, daylight or artificial), microscopic life is born which is green in colour; suspended in the water this causes it to turn green, or it can settle to become green slime over the sand, rocks, plants, grass, etc., or even as green strips on the sides. The fish will thrive on the green algae, unless excessive, as is emphasised in Chapter 7, but not 'blanketweed' described in the section on ponds.

Nevertheless, green is not pleasant to view and should not be permitted in a show tank. The cure is simple: cut down the amount of light received by the aquarium, whether that light be sunlight, daylight or artificial light. Of course, if the light is reduced too much the plants will not grow. The green algae already formed can be cleared in a few days by using proprietary algicides available from your aquarium dealer; after this period, there should be no need to do more than change one third of the water, by siphoning off from the bottom to remove the dead algae before it pollutes the tank. If no fish are present, a swarm of *Daphnia* will soon clean the tank by the simple method of eating all the algae. Strongly growing plants, and general cleanliness, make it more difficult for algae to appear in the tank.

Should the water turn yellow, however, the process has been carried too far, and the water must be changed; the sudden death of the microscopic green algae, due, say, to heat, causes them to decompose and turn the water yellow, which means that the water is now foul and must be changed most urgently as even half an hour can be fatal.

Unsuspected Dangers

1.   Incorrect feeding, especially through lack of live foods or their substitutes. See pages 36–37 for details.

2.   Bad condition of the tank:

   (a) Fish overcrowded? Too many (or too big) fish can be crammed into a tank for a while but sooner or later will fall sick.

   (b) Dirt in a tank aggravates overcrowding. Excess food is nearly always the cause of dirt that lies about the tank as brown sediment. In bad instances the gravel becomes black.

(c) If the aquarium temperature is consistently kept too high, or too low, the fish will be weakened, even to the point of sickness and of death.

(d) Too strong or too prolonged a light shining on the tank can be as tiring for fish as for humans. They, too, need some shade or at least some periods of darkness (say, at night). Shelter can be provided by floating plants or by rocks arranged in the form of a bridge or of a T. Furthermore, fish that are feeling out of sorts will be able to retire into these places for rest and privacy.

(e) The plants should be healthy and be sufficient in number to do their work properly.

(f) Bad conditions encourage secondary infections; for instance, fighting between incompatible or sparring species can lead to open wounds or split fins which then become infected. Be careful only to keep compatible species together. Some marine fish can only be kept as isolated specimens in a community collection if fighting is to be avoided.

3. The presence of paint (even in the house next door), varnish, strong bath salts, disinfectants, strong smelling oil-containing matter, some kitchen smells, are definitely harmful as the water absorbs these foreign elements to the distress of the fish. The importance of this point can be underlined by the following cases, all of which were true situations.

(a) The aquarium was kept near a bathroom where strong disinfectant was used for ten days; the fish fell ill.

(b) The chauffeur used to feed the fish and to rearrange the rocks; he came straight from the garage and his hands smelt of petrol and oil.

(c) The room had beautiful parquet flooring which was regularly polished; the accumulative effect of the polish smell was too much for the tank.

(d) The over-careful aquarist who washed his hands thoroughly before touching the tank; unfortunately he used strongly scented soap.

The above are mere examples; they show the attention that must be paid to this point. In nearly every case, however, a tell-tale scum (often oily) on the top of the aquarium water indicated the cause of the trouble, but this does not always apply; some disinfectants leave virtually no scum.

The top of the water will have to be skimmed, and even part changed (with water of the same temperature) as detailed earlier in this chapter (pages 31–32), until about one third of the water *from the top* has been removed – if possible without being stirred. A further protection is to cover the top of the aquarium with a sheet of glass or some such substitute until the danger has passed.

4. Harmful substances introduced into the tank from outside. Apart from the non-aquatic rocks, ornaments, etc., these can be brought into the tank by dirty hands, newly applied nail varnish, dirty cloths, dusters or tools that have been kept in a drawer with tins of paint, etc. It is surprising how strongly the hands can smell of the kitchen, the garage, or of a tin of varnish.

5. Disease introduced by new fish, plants, or live foods. Unsuitable fish can engender disease if they take up too much oxygen because they are too big, or are fish more used to the running water of streams (in the case of coldwater fish); some types of fish, too, do not live quietly in a community tank and are bullies or even killers. Fish accustomed to aeration will suffer in still water.

6. Something wrong with the water temperature, especially in the case of tropicals; too wide fluctuations, faulty wiring, or

perhaps simply that the heater unit has got buried by disturbed gravel. Perhaps, too, the heater has failed altogether – not always noticeable in centrally heated rooms. Some thermometers are not quite as reliable as one would like and they, too, should be checked in case they are giving false readings.

7.   Water enemies, as described in Chapter 6, should not be in the tank.

8.   Fish urine is not visible but results in excess toxic ammonia compounds which affect the gill plates of the fish, causing red inflammation and ultra-quick breathing. The fish hangs at unusual angles, even quivers, and later has blotches on its body. Water must be changed urgently, filters cleaned and aeration increased.

9.   An imbalance of plant life usually shows as: (a) Patches of black gravel developing round the plant roots because of harmful nitrates or (b) White precipitate grains forming on the leaves during the night and disappearing gradually by day. In both cases, the balance of the tank is altogether too precarious because there are either too many fish for the few plants, or the reverse. Even one extra hour of sunlight or a few extra grains of dirt (e.g. food) could cause havoc in this situation. Change the water, get more plants (or fish) and adjust the duration/ strength of the top lighting to encourage plant growth. A slight increase of ten per cent growth may correct matters.

If the tank water is too acid, as shown by a pH reading (percentage of hydrogen) of below 7.0 on the test kits widely available in the shops, then a plant fertiliser should be used.

In marine aquaria, there is a tendency over a period of time for pH to fall. Regular partial water changes with replacement synthetic water of the correct SG will prevent this happening. Again, using a pH test kit will alert you to this occurrence.

10.   In addition to the pH factor of acidity/alkalinity just mentioned, is the DH factor or 'degree of hardness' of the water. Waters vary widely: for example, at Manaus on the River Negro in South America, where so many Neons and

Cardinal fish come from, the DH is 4–6; in London it is 12–18. A sudden transfer at the end of an aeroplane journey to a totally different DH throws such a strain on the delicately balanced membranes of the fish gill plates that they collapse and the fish usually dies in less than an hour – the actual time depending on the violence of the fluctuation.

11.   Water stratification means that there are insufficient fish and/or aeration to give an even, all over temperature, so that fish are being forced to go through different strata of temperatures as they swim up or down. Particularly vulnerable are the base dwellers like the Catfish who normally stay in the bottom 3cm of water. Make quite sure that the heater reaches down to the lower levels of the tank which are therefore heated. Alternatively, adjust your aeration.

12.   Is your filter clean? Is it big enough? Is the rate of flow fast enough, or are there too many eddies and unswept areas? A dirty filter merely pours black poisoned water, making matters worse.

13.   Is there sufficient overhead shade/protection from the toplight? Are there enough nooks, crannies, clefts, ledges, covers, plant thickets, thick-leaved plants? You need to cater for all types, including the weak, timid and infirm.

14. Signs of fish distress

    (a) Drooping the fins, pale colour (fear/pain often intensifies colour patterns unnaturally), lack of appetite, lethargy.
        Conversely, drooping fins on a marine fish is not necessarily a sign of illness; many swim with fins folded as a matter of course.

    (b) Head/tail hanging down, moping off into unusual parts of the tank (top swimmers coming down to mid water, etc.), hiding in plants (often head first), making slow circles at the surface, tail down and mouth up, seeking more oxygen (change water at once).

(c) Unusual darting to safety, panting, shivering, trying to bury and hide, or keeping mouth open for too long. (Act at once to help. If you can't do better at least change the water.)

Or else:

(d) Pining. Never keep shoaling fish as solitary specimens. Your fish may want a mate. It may be psychologically upset and want a home of its own: a cave, cleft, or a thick leaf, etc.

(e) Boisterousness and bullying. Persistent bullies can be temporarily isolated in a breeding trap or clean jam jar filled with tank water and floating on the tank water surface. It may just want better, more varied foods. Constipation shows as long, thread-like excreta hanging down from the vent – give (laxative) live *Daphnia* foods.

15. Try to understand your fish
They do their very best to tell you their preferences, to make friends with you, and to help you to realise that their shapes and colours are positive clues to their ideal environment. As you are responsible for their well-being, please note the following points:

(a) Body long, slim and torpedo-shaped. A fast/far swimmer needing lots of free space.

(b) Torpedo body, but with prominent finnage. A quick accelerator which will dart out to forage rather than go in for far-ranging swims. Less free space, frequently interspersed with foliage, would be preferred.

(c) Eyes clear, prominent, perhaps rimmed with a strong colour (like red, for instance). The waters would need to be clean and clear for all-round vision. Brightly lit. Murky, cloudy tanks are no more welcome to them and no more conducive to good health than persistent smog is to us.

(d) Longitudinal, light sheeny markings on the body. Require both free space and strong currents (so step up aeration). The light sheen calls for clean and bright soft waters (nicely filtered, and of DH 6–8 rather than 12–18). Often the digestive tracts are short, so food is eliminated quickly – which means that the fish should be fed three times a day. The strong currents of the filters should eliminate all droppings quickly.

(e) High body colours, like the Neon, the Cardinal, the Glowlight. Their native habitat of shallow streams is rich with fallen vegetation, over which flow pronounced currents creating DH 4–6 and pH 6.8 with very low parts per million of dissolved solids. Their high body colours are perfect camouflage in the piercing shafts of strong sunlight which break through the overhanging vegetation. So please reproduce overhanging protection, and alternating light and shade.

(f) Smudged, but high-coloured body markings, like the Rosy Barb, the Purple Headed Barb, the Tiger Barb. Similar to the above Neons, these fish need overhead vegetation, but not quite so thickly hung, to give areas of light and shade, rather than piercing shafts. Less timid than the Neons, the Barbs like to move into a brightly lit area and bask/browse for a while before returning to the shade. The less fastidious fish (indicated by untidy smudges and less clean-cut markings) is more able to endure poor diets and survive better in murky waters.

(g) Rounded Body. The rounder the body, the deeper the waters required; examples are Scats and Angels. Also indicates a fish which sallies forth from protective clefts or reed thickets, rather than staying in the open for prolonged periods. If either of the fish mentioned becomes aggressive then you have upset it psychologically by not providing a home of its own, or by depriving it of congenial mates. Its built-in shyness then turns to aggressive defensiveness. But there are differences. The Scats have smudged untidy markings indicating wide tolerance to varied waters, and can go from full marine, through brackish, to fresh waters. The clean-cut, bright sheeny Angels, with clear eyes rimmed with red, denote a more evolved fish requiring full freshwater conditions only.

The differences continue with feeding habits: the Scat has a lack of discrimination in the choice of food and is gluttonous, constantly foraging and eating anything/anywhere. The Angel, with its smaller mouth, picks daintily at chosen morsels and has been known to go on hunger strike if not given satisfactory food (try live foods to tempt them out of their obstinacy). If their characteristic long, delicate trailing ventral fins become split and frayed, then poor tank conditions must be improved, otherwise infection will set in.

(h) Barbels. Koi, and the previously mentioned Barbs, have barbels (fleshy whiskers at the corner of the mouth) and forage to the point of greed. They therefore excrete a lot and often, and soon foul the aquarium; your filter will need to be efficient to cope with this.

(i) Mouth. If forward-pointing (terminal), then the fish tends to be a mid-water dweller. Upward-pointing (super terminal) and downward-pointing (sub terminal) denote the top and bottom waters preferred respectively. Hatchets, for example, with their strong pectoral (breast) fins, super terminal mouths and flat backs, not only swim on top, they will readily leap along (or even above) the surface to catch their food. Hence their tanks need to be covered about 8cm above the water surface to prevent them from jumping out. Barbels around the mouth are used to locate food by bottom-dwelling species. Aggressive mouths denote danger to others. Strong suckers on the mouth indicate an ability to hang or suck along as they feed off ledges, rocks, plants or glass and to withstand strong currents as they cling. Fast-flowing aeration is helpful. Most sucker mouths are used to feed off green algae, which is produced by strong light, so that requirement must be provided. Such vegetarians dislike meat.

(j) Backs and tummy. The more arching the back and the flatter the tummy, the more the fish will stay down at the bottom – look at the extreme example of the Catfish. Note that the clearer, more finely marked Leopard Catfish requires clean waters and less base mulm/debris than the darkly smudged varieties. The more arched the back is, the slower a swimmer the fish will be. Some are seldom capable of more than a darting acceleration for a short burst.

(k) Eyes. The wider apart they are, the less light they like and they are more likely to be crepuscular – dawn or dusk seeing them venture out – like the Sucking Catfish, the Plecostomus (now *Hypostomus* sp). Many Catfish hide up by day amongst rocks or well-placed pieces of plastic pipe or overturned flowerpots. Such fish benefit from a feed just after 'lights out'.

(l) Killifish, such as the *Aphyosemion* species, have excessive high colours and finnage. They live and die in excessive haste, as birth, maturity, spawning and death all have to be crowded into a few short months when the rains fill the mud pools and before the sun dries them out.

(m) Marine Fish. You must choose species carefully. Many

are best kept as isolated specimens whilst other require certain other inhabitants in the tank to make them feel at home – a good example of this is the Clownfish who appreciates the presence of the Sea-anemone. Some marine fishes are not always safe with smaller species or marine invertebrates.

General Body Appearance Of Defence Or Of Attack

If the mouth is small and the body is laterally compressed with long feelers and camouflaged colours (rather than of garish colouring like the Dwarf Gourami), the fish is likely to prefer to shoal for defence and would wilt if left alone, especially if unprotected by rock clefts or reed thickets.

If, like the Black Widow, the mouth is businesslike but the body has heavy finnage trailing downwards, then it is likely to be a mid-water dweller which stays under protective large/broad/wide leaves to sally forth for food. It snaps back firmly in self-defence and does not depend so much on shoaling; but stops well short of being aggressive. If your particular specimen is over-liable to snap, then what are you doing wrong? The fault will be yours, not that of the fish.

Conclusion

Every word of the above points is important. For instance, one very competent aquarist who had 'green-fingers', and could keep fish without trouble, suddenly found things going all wrong; the fish were not over-crowded, were well-fed, in a long-established and correctly balanced tank, beautifully clean, the plants were thriving, nothing new had been introduced for two months, and yet something was wrong. No, there had been no paint, disinfectant or varnish used – the aquarist was quite, quite sure. In the end, the cause of the trouble was found: aquarium tools were being kept in a drawer with long-forgotten, half-empty tins of paint. When there is trouble, there *is* a cause, no matter how obscure, and it can be found and remedied.

In general, the aquarium which has been expertly set up in the first place should seldom go wrong.

The causes of trouble detailed here are out-of-the-ordinary ones. It is quite untrue to maintain that a bar, a public house, a busy hotel foyer, or any other crowded place is unsuitable for an aquarium. They continue to be found in such places, and in more rigorous conditions such as the toy departments of famous stores – even at Christmas time – and at exhibitions, where literally thousands of people crowd past every hour of the day for weeks on end, and when the heat and the dust are so bad that the staff in charge of the exhibitions have to be changed every few hours to avoid headaches and sore throats. And yet the fish do not suffer. So, given a fair chance and proper knowledge, fish will prove themselves trouble-free, hardy and a source of great pleasure.

5

CLEANING THE TANK AND GENERAL INFORMATION

Keeping the tank clean is very important and quite simple, provided specialist advice is followed. Annoyingly enough, this advice consists mainly of a series of 'don'ts', all elaborated elsewhere but grouped below for the sake of convenience. Numbers 2 and 3 are especially important.

1. Don't buy your fish from a dealer whom you distrust or whose technical knowledge *as an aquarist* you feel is insufficient. (See pages 8–10.)
2. Don't buy too many fish or too few plants so that the balance of your tank is upset. (See pages 13 and 20.)
3. Don't, please don't, overfeed, particularly with dried foods (page 34), but live food or a varied diet is very helpful.
4. Place the aquarium in a sensible position; not backing on to a window (page 18), not in too bright a spot (page 15), not in a strong draught unless your dealer has been warned of that and has provided strong heaters.
5. Siphon off the bottom occasionally (pages 31–32), and wipe the inside of the glass very, very gently.
6. Regularly monitor the water temperature in tropical tanks. Marine aquaria require more regular checks in order to maintain exact water conditions. As well as temperature, check also pH and SG and, especially in the first few weeks following setting up, the levels of ammonia and

nitrite so that fish can be introduced with the minimum of stress.

7. Please re-read No. 15 on understanding your fish (pages 44–48).

General Information
In the limited scope of this book, there are several subjects that cannot be dealt with fully, and yet they ought at least to be mentioned. Accordingly, they are given below in the form of notes.

Classification Of Fish
The hundreds of fish suitable for an aquarium are divided into Orders, the Orders into Families, the Families into Genera, and the Genera into Species. The most important order is Ostariophysi which contains the families of Characins (Black Widows, Beacons, Flames, Neons), of Carps (all the live bearers, Harlequins, Barbs, White Cloud Mountain Minnows), of Loaches (Kuhli Loach) and of Catfish (Glass Catfish, Sucking Catfish, etc.)

The Fins On A Fish
Most fish have seven fins of which four are paired, namely the pectoral or breast, and the ventral or pelvic; the eighth fin is called the adipose and is found mostly in Characins and in Catfish. (See fig. 5 overleaf.)

Community Fish
All those described in this book are community fish; that means that they will live peacefully together. There are at least four hundred types of these. The non-community fish are not dealt with here.

Labyrinthfishes (Gouramies, etc.) need air above the water surface, which they store in a special breathing organ, or they drown – note this when carrying them home.

The Kinds Of Water
In different localities, water varies very considerably. Quite apart from the question of being hard or soft, the actual

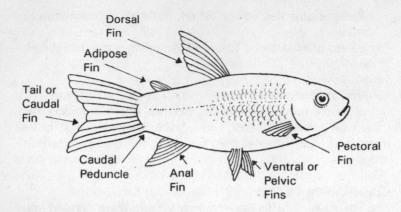

Fig. 5 The Fins on a Fish

composition of the water varies with the amounts of salts, minerals and other such substances dissolved in it. Special Test Kits are sold for measuring pH. Unless the reader is seriously preparing to breed the more difficult kinds of fish, he need not concern himself with this question at all.

pH denotes the degree of acidity or alkalinity of the water and is measured on the following scale; the abbreviation pH denoting the percentage of 'Hydrogen ion concentration'.

acid ———————— neutral ———— alkaline

6.0 6.2 6.4 6.6 6.8   7.0   7.2 7.4 7.6 7.8 8.0

Sodium bicarbonate added to the water will make it alkaline; acid sodium phosphate or very heavily diluted hydrochloric acid has the opposite effect.

Water that has remained quite untouched is likely to give different pH readings at different times of the day because interaction of the chemicals contained in it is always taking place. Further, an amount of water of pH 6.5 mixed with an equal quantity of pH 7.5 does not necessarily give a reading of pH 7.0 because one water may be 'buffered'. 'Buffered' water has a high mineral content and the influence of all these dissolved solids has to be overcome before there is an alteration of the pH reading. Tap water and rain water are not usually 'buffered'.

DH (or degree of hardness) should also be noted, and it can easily be determined by one of the speciality kits widely sold. Basically, the wild fish come from soft waters DH 2–8; home-bred town fish can be as high as DH 18. The adaptability of fish to this factor is enormous provided the fluctuation is done gradually, i.e. at least over some hours, if not days. 'When in doubt, soften the water' is a useful adage.

'Parts per million' of known salts/chemical content is a further refinement, but requires fairly elaborate equipment to determine/maintain and is beyond the scope of this book.

Fluoride in drinking water is becoming increasingly common. Boiling the water does not remove it, nor does ordinary filtration.

Water for marine aquaria is made up by mixing tap water with a 'salt mix' available from your aquatic dealer. It must be made to an exact condition, which can be verified by its Specific Gravity with an aquarium hydrometer. Replacement synthetic seawater for partial water changes must be made to the same specifications of SG and temperature as those in the main aquarium. But, remember when 'topping up' the marine tank to replace water loss through evaporation, only fresh water should be used as 'salts' are not lost during evaporation.

Measuring The Capacity Of A Tank

The capacity of an aquarium can be found in gallons by multiplying in feet the length x breadth x height x 6¼. For example, an aquarium 2 ft x 1 ft x 1 ft holds 12½ gallons. This can be roughly converted into litres by multiplying by 4½.

One gallon of water has 90,000 drops, weighs 10 lb and exerts pressure on the inside of the aquarium glass of 10 lb per square inch. (All these figures are approximate.) Metrically, this would be approximately equal to 4.5 kilogrammes per 6.4 square centimetres.

Sealing A Tank

Modern all-glass tanks should not leak; however, it may be prudent to re-seal, say, secondhand tanks, just to be on the safe side. Silicone sealer should be applied in a continuous bead around all interior seams, having first dried out the tank thoroughly and cleaned surfaces with methylated spirit. Do use silicone sealant in a well-ventilated atmosphere; the sealant normally 'cures' in 24 hours.

Use only sealants specially made for aquarium use. No, this isn't a blatant commercial. Your fish will die from fungus inhibitors found in cheaper, non-aquarium-use forms such as bathroom sealants – you have been warned!

Conversion Factors

1 gallon = 4.546 litres
1 pound = 0.4536 kilogrammes
1 inch = 2.54 centimetres

To work out Centigrade temperatures in Fahrenheit, divide by 5, multiply by 9, and add 32. The answer will be the number of degrees Fahrenheit.

For example: 45°C = 113°F

$$\frac{45}{5} \times \frac{9}{1} + 32 = 113°F$$

6

WATER ENEMIES AND DISEASES
(TROPICAL AND COLDWATER)

The great danger when catching live foods for a pond or aquarium, or when procuring plants from untried sources, is that water enemies will be introduced as well; these are small aquatic insects which can kill or harm baby fish and, in at least two instances, even medium-sized adult fish. The main water enemies are the Water Tigers, Dragon Fly larvae and *Hydra*.

The Water Tiger is a long, thin insect, shaped rather like a caterpillar, and has two vicious pincers with which it can hold its victim and through which it can suck its blood. It grows to 4cm or more, but probably its most dangerous size is half-grown, as it is then difficult to detect. A good swimmer, it can tackle and kill fish twice its own size.

The Dragon Fly Larva is similar to the Water Tiger except that it does not swim much but lies in wait for its prey. The victims are merely held by the pincers and are then destroyed by its hard mouth, which can do amazing damage even through the sturdy scale protection of quite big fish.

Hydra is different from the two described above, being very much smaller and capable of harming only fry. Its presence is betrayed by a group or bunch of thread-like streamers or hairs hanging in the water; these are the tentacles. Each *Hydra* is roughly 2cm long, having about half a dozen tentacles spread out like a star fish. Since it invariably seems to multiply rapidly, ways have had to be found to remove the vast numbers other than by emptying and cleaning the pond or aquarium.

The aquarium can be purified by raising the temperature to 38°C for twenty to thirty minutes (no fish being present, of course), or by introducing Blue or Leeri Gourami fish, which will eat the *Hydra* when forced to do so by sheer hunger – so they should not be fed by the aquarist in the meantime. These allies can be obtained from your dealer and are best in the normal home tank. Some English water snails (*Lymnaea stagnalis*) will also eat *Hydra*, but they have the bad habit of eating plants as well.

One more way of eliminating *Hydra*, this time without having to remove the fish, is to black out the tank entirely – tops, sides and bottom – leaving only a 5cm x 5cm gap on the side facing the light. Within a few hours, all the *Hydra* in the dark tank will have gathered on the 5cm x 5cm opening and can then easily be wiped off with a sponge.

For the pond, one quarter of a grain of potassium permanganate can be added for each 4.5 litres of water; if no fry are present at the time the dose can be doubled. This should be left for two or three days and the water then gradually changed until half or two thirds of the original has been replaced. The fish need not be removed. Another alternative remedy for the *Hydra*-infected pond is ammonium sulphate added to the water at the rate of 1 teaspoonful to every 45 litres; this also will destroy the enemies but not the fish.

These three then – Water Tiger, Dragon Fly Larvae and *Hydra* – are the main water enemies, but the list is by no means exhausted. Some 'foreign' creatures are, however, quite harmless and are rapidly eaten by such fish as the Barbs, who seem to enjoy the change of diet.

The obvious moral is not to introduce these pests in the first place! This cannot be guaranteed, of course, but the practised eye of an expert can afford fairly sure protection as he will take every care to screen his live foods and plants before selling them to the public. The same remarks apply forcefully to the diseases described below; indeed, they serve to emphasise why the isolation of fish, stressed in Chapter 1, is so very necessary.

Diseases

The diseases are divided into two groups: Tropical and Coldwater, not because there is a cut-and-dried distinction between them, but because they apply more often to the class of fish under which they are listed. The suggested cures and symptoms apply to both classes. Obviously all nets, instruments, etc., should be sterilised after use to prevent the spread of infection from the isolation tank.

Introduction To Treatment

It is usual to treat the whole aquarium for any outbreak of a commonly-shared disease, whilst treatments for individual fish suffering, say, from wounds or split fins, can be undertaken in a separate 'hospital' tank. The secret of successful treatment depends on correct diagnosis of the disease in the first place. Always remove any activated carbon from filters before adding medication – carbon will adsorb the medication before it can get to work on the disease! Also it is a good idea to increase aeration, as many medications use up oxygen as they work.

Many treatments are copper-based which, in most cases, make them unsafe to use in marine aquariums, especially if invertebrates are present.

After treatment (successful or not) make a partial water change and replace carbon in the filter to remove any trace of medication from the water.

Starting with the Tropicals:
White Spot *(Ichthyophthiriasis)*

This disease is encountered by everyone who keeps fish: it is probably the aquatic equivalent of our common cold, or flu, as most fish seem to suffer from it at one time or another; theories abound about the disease lying dormant in every aquarium just waiting for an advantageous time to strike at any fish weakened by stress, or a chill – sometimes the addition of new fish may trigger off an outbreak even though both newcomer and existing stock are, in themselves, quite healthy. However, just as our ailments can be easily treated, so too can White Spot.

These parasites look like tiny white dots on (not in) the fish, usually showing first on the tail or behind the eyes. The parasite (*Ichthyophthirius multifilis*) has a complicated life-style: a period when it is seen on the fish, a period as a dormant cyst on the tank floor, and a free-swimming period as it seeks a new host. It is only during the free-swimming period that it can be attacked by aquarium remedies. White Spot is a highly contagious disease and will spread rapidly to all fish if not treated as soon as it is noticed.

As the parasite is fish-dependent, one could argue that leaving the aquarium devoid of fish for a week or so would effect a cure, but who would wish to deny the beauty of the aquarium even for that short length of time – and how would you know if the tank was clear of the disease when you put them back?

With growing restrictions on public acquisition of chemi-cals from the pharmacist, it is easier to rely on proprietary treatments from your aquatic dealer. All are extremely effec-tive and usually work within a few days at the most; it is no longer necessary to raise the water temperature during treat-ment except, perhaps, where fishes intolerant to remedies are involved (Loaches, some naked Catfish, for instance). Here, raising the temperature to 32°C for a few hours every few days may eventually damage the parasite without weakening the fish. Because some remedies colour the water, you should be prepared for the aquarium plants to be set back a little (the remedy cuts down the amount of light reaching them); at the end of the treatment period it is usual either to carry out a regular partial water change, or use a carbon filter medium, to remove the medication from the water. Incidentally, always remove any carbon filter medium from filters during the period of treatments, as the carbon will remove the medication before it has time to work.

It is useful to know the water capacity of each of your tanks, as dosage with remedies (for whatever disease) has to be accurate to effect a successful cure: underdosing won't do the trick, overdosing can be dangerous to the fish. Follow manu-facturers' instructions implicitly; adding that bit extra 'for luck' is tempting providence too much.

Marine White Spot, *Cryptocaryon irritans*, is, as its common name suggests, the saltwater aquarium's equivalent of *Ichthyophthiriasis*. The symptoms are similar with the tiny white spots identifying the disease. Proprietary remedies are effective as is the use of UV sterilisers.

Velvet

The symptoms are similar to White Spot but the fish looks as if it has a dusty covering rather than the more easily seen spots of the previous disease. The parasite is known as *Oodinium*, and the remedy follows the same procedure as with the preceding disease. Mildly affected fish can be treated in the main aquarium; more badly afflicted cases should be treated in isolation in a separate hospital tank.

Marine Velvet, *Amyloodinium ocellatum*, is a literally irritating disease causing the fish to scratch against obstacles in the aquarium to acquire relief. The small spots are much smaller than those of Marine White Spot. Again, proprietary remedies are effective if the disease is diagnosed early enough.

Flukes

This is an irritant disease caused by at least two parasites; one (*Gyrodactylus*) is known as Skin Flukes, and provokes the usual reaction to irritation; that is, the fish rubs itself against the rocks or sides of the aquarium and darts at high speed only to stop suddenly. The other parasite, Gill Flukes (*Dactylogyrus*), attacks the gill membranes and causes the fish to breathe extra rapidly and even pant at the surface as if oxygen levels are low; the latter may not be the case, merely the inflamed gills cannot make use of what oxygen there is. (On the other hand, don't leap to a hasty conclusion: check tank conditions for poor water quality before deciding that it's Gill Flukes!) Both types of Flukes are highly contagious. A further gill parasite, the Gill Maggot (*Ergasilus*), also signals its presence by the same 'difficulty in breathing' behaviour.

Short-term baths (20–30 minutes, or far less if visible distress occurs) in various solutions can be tried, ranging from salt (rock salt, not table salt), formalin, ammonium hydroxide,

Trypaflavine, and other antibacterial types. Take advice from your dealer or even a veterinary surgeon, as many compounds are only available on prescription. Gill and Skin Flukes are also common in marine situations. In this case, a freshwater bath can be effective as well as proprietary medications.

Shimmies

In this, the fish sways rapidly from side to side and yet does not move forward even though it appears to be 'swimming'. These shakings are easily recognised.

The cause is either a chill or unsuitable aquarium water which has become poisoned by excess urine, by harmful nitrites (as distinct from nitrates), toxic substances transferred into the water by air or by hand, or by plain old-fashioned dirt.

The cure is to raise the temperature to 31°C, for seven to twelve days, and to change the water with 'old' water – that is water that has been standing for 36 to 48 hours. Feed well on live foods in the meantime. Aerate.

Dropsy

Dropsy causes the scales of the fish to stick out in a most repulsive, bloated fashion. Mild cases, which are strongly suspected of being a form of indigestion, are sometimes cured by a 4-hour bath in a solution of 2 level teaspoons of Epsom Salts per 4.5 litres of water (of the same temperature as that in the tank). The cause of Dropsy is thought to be a worm in the intestines, but what makes it attack particular fish is not known.

Attempts to cure Dropsy include first improving overall aquarium conditions, then/or isolating infected fish to a separate aquarium. Sometimes Dropsy is quite contagious, sometimes only one fish suffers. Although draining off the built-up body fluid with a hypodermic needle is sometimes advocated, this practice cannot be recommended to anyone other than those qualified to do so; the slightest misplacement of the needle will physically harm the fish. The use of antibiotics may prove successful but these need veterinary guidance.

Wasting Disease

This is what the name implies. The fish begins to waste away, starting from the tail, and becomes miserably thin, finally dying. Various theories are advanced in explanation: the fish is old; the general tank conditions are poor (Chapter 4); or the fish was forced-bred (Chapter 1). All these can be true in part, but none fully explains this puzzling disease. The symptoms are also similar to those of Fish Tuberculosis, but in either event once the fish reaches such advanced physical debilitation there is little that can be done for it.

The above diseases attack tropicals more frequently than they do coldwater fish, for whom the main ones are as follows:

Fungus

A white cotton-wool-like smudge appears on parts of the fish, and is easily recognised. The effect, by *Saprolegnia* bacteria, is triggered very often by bad conditions, such as overcrowding, poor feeding, or prolonged low temperature, etc., as detailed in Chapter 4. Bruises and knocks can sometimes also begin the ailment, which is highly contagious. Obviously, the suspected bad conditions must first be remedied to prevent a recurrence or a spread of the disease.

The cure is one that applies very frequently to coldwater fish, and one that can perhaps be used even where the complaint cannot be diagnosed and an 'anything is better than nothing' policy is felt advisable. This salt treatment is accordingly described in detail.

Salt Treatment

Rock salt, or, failing that, cooking salt, should be used; table salt is not safe as it contains chemicals to keep it dry and powdery. There are two methods of application, somewhat conflicting, so both are described here. The first is the older, conventional one; the second is the newer.

METHOD 1

Place the fish in 'old' water of the same temperature as the tank and add 2 level teaspoons of rock salt per 4.5 litres and leave for a day.

During the next day, slowly build up the dose to 4 level teaspoons, and finally on the third day to 6 level teaspoons of rock salt per 4.5 litres of water.

By now, the fish should be cured and 'old' water of the same temperature can be added until the salt content has been eliminated. Should the cure need to be prolonged beyond three days, a new saline solution should be made as the other will have tended to become stale.

METHOD 2

This is a four-day cure, by giving the fish four baths, one a day, in a saline solution freshly made each day; the fish is to be left in the bath for four hours daily before being transferred back into fresh water. Great care *must* be taken that there is no difference in the water temperatures when the fish is transferred from the salt to the fresh and vice versa. This point is of the utmost importance, otherwise the fish will be harmed, not helped, by these salt baths. The fish should be excited as little as possible while being caught in a net to be transferred from one water to the other.

The strength of the saline solution is:

1st day: 2 heaped teaspoons of rock
        or cooking salt per 4.5 litres.
2nd day: 4 heaped teaspoons.
3rd day: 4 heaped teaspoons.
4th day: 2 heaped teaspoons.

Feed the fish well each time on its return to fresh water; keep it in dim light during treatment.

Alternative Treatments

Drugs like Phenoxethol are the basis for many patented medicines sold to cure fungus. The following do-it-yourself ones could be tried.

Swab with iodine, or mercurochrome, or merthiolate, *all diluted 1000 times* (i.e. 1cc in a litre of water). Alternatively, add these in two or three doses to the tank (changing the water after cure).

For more stubborn cases: Potassium dichromate (2½ grains per 4.5 litres), Phenoxethol (dilute 1cc per litre), and then give

10 to 40 drops per 4.5 litres); Malachite green (¼ grain to 4.5 litres); Terramycin (50–200 milligrammes per 4.5 litres, in several stages), or Sulphamerazine sodium (4 grains per 4.5 litres). **Always dissolve medicants before adding to the aquarium**.

Always administer medicines in several stages, in case your tank water over-reacts; disconnect all carbon medium filtration; keep the tank in dim light; aerate it; feed the fish with live foods; allow no dirt; change the tank water at the finish of the treatment.

A much more drastic treatment, which can be tried in 'kill or cure' attempts, is a solution of 10 drops of ammonia in 4.5 litres of water, leaving the fish in it for not more than five minutes; if, however, the fish begins to show signs of acute distress, and starts losing its balance and turning on its side, it should be removed at once.

Just as freshwater fish suffering from parasitic attacks can benefit from a saltwater bath, so marine fish can find relief from similar attacks by being given a brief bath in *fresh* water. Again, the length of the bath should be judged accurately, with the affected fish being removed at the first sign of distress and returned to salt water again.

Tail Rot and Fin Congestion

These are two separate diseases, both caused by bad conditions (Chapter 4) or by a sharp fall of temperature. The symptoms are blood-red streaks or veins appearing on the fins or tails, which will drop and crumple.

The cure is the fungus treatment already described. At the same time, steps should be taken to improve the water conditions in the aquarium to prevent these secondary infections recurring.

A more drastic cure is to hold the fish gently but firmly in a damp cloth and to cut off the affected parts, afterwards disinfecting the wound with a pink solution of potassium permanganate.

Alternatively, the diseased parts can be burned off with a 50% solution of hydrogen peroxide; once the affected parts have been dripped in this solution they will fall away about 48 hours after the fish has been returned to the aquarium.

There remain three main diseases to which both tropicals and coldwater fish are equally prone:

Constipation

This is indicated by long excreta threads hanging from the fish and by a general bloated appearance of the body.

The cure is to leave the fish for 4 hours in a solution of Epsom Salts (1 heaped teaspoon to 4.5 litres of water) or feed with live *Daphnia*.

Swim Bladder Trouble

Fish have a swim bladder filled with a gas and regulated so that they can rest in comfort at any angle and at any depth. If this gas pressure is not exactly right, the fish will stay at the top and have difficulty in reaching the bottom of the tank; or, conversely, will stay at the bottom and have to make strenuous efforts to rise – only to sink again when exhausted.

Mild attacks are sometimes caused by indigestion, and the constipation treatment mentioned above might help. Relief can also be given by placing the fish in shallow water of a very slightly higher temperature, e.g. rather less than 1°C. Although uncomfortable, the fish is not in pain and there is no need to destroy it, particularly as the disease is not contagious.

Swim bladder trouble is very often the result of a sharp temperature change, particularly if the fish has been taken from one container and put in another without the temperature of the two waters being equalised beforehand. Sometimes a cure can be effected by giving the fish a 4-hour bath in a mixture of sodium acid phosphate and of household ammonia, at a strength of 1 flat teaspoon of sodium acid phosphate and 5 drops of household ammonia to 54 litres of water. But the mixture must be freshly made. Obviously, too, the mixture must be the same temperature as the aquarium water.

Pop Eyes, Bruises, General Protuberances

When the eyes stick out and swell, or swellings appear on the body as a result of bruises, etc., a certain amount of hit-or-miss treatment can be employed. If these symptoms are the result of internal disorders they are virtually incurable as so little is know about them. However, when they are the results of external blows or cuts, the affected parts could be gently wiped with cotton wool soaked in a strong solution of boracic acid (at the rate of 3 heaped teaspoons per 4.5 litres of water). Alternatively, a mixture of 1 drop of iodine and 10 drops of glycerine could be used. The fish should then be left alone for a week to await results.

When the protuberances are caused by parasites lodging under the skin, the fish can be held in a damp cloth and have the affected spots touched with one drop of purple solution of potassium permanganate with 1 drop of 2% Mercurochrome. Potassium permanganate at this strength will burn the skin of the fish and should be applied only to the exact spot of the protuberance; if this is not large or severe, the Mercurochrome treatment should be enough by itself.

A subsequent bath for 4 hours in a salt solution of 2 heaped teaspoons of rock or cooking salt per 4.5 litres of water is beneficial.

Alternatively, a bath for 5 minutes in a solution of 1 teaspoon of TCP disinfectant to each ½ litre of water will kill most lice without harming the fish; if the fish starts to heel over on to its side, however, it should be returned at once to fresh water of the same temperature.

Conclusion

Whether a fish is sick or just 'feeling off colour', the following points will help both coldwater and tropical fish.

A change of water and of surroundings, by transference to another tank, often acts as a tonic – more especially if the new tank has green water. As always, care must be taken to equalise temperatures before transference.

The addition of aeration, or, in the case of coldwater especially, of very gently running water, has the same effect as taking a city man to the seaside or for a short holiday.

Dim light, shallow water, and live food are all three a great help. The chemicals mentioned (potassium permanganate, salt, etc.) should first be dissolved in a little water before being used;

they should never be dropped in as solids in fish water and allowed to dissolve there, because the act of dissolution sets up very strong local chemical reactions and liberates strong gases.

Finally, a plea for restraint must be made. The difference between 'leave well alone' and 'too late to cure' is finely shaded and it is a question of some judgment when or whether to begin a cure for a suspected disease. After all, there still is a strong moral in the story of the healthy man who began to read medical books; studying the various symptoms he convinced himself he suffered from each and every disease (except housemaid's knee), until he had to visit his doctor for a course of reassurance!

New Medicines

These improve daily, especially as the veterinary profession is now becoming involved in the aquarium trade, and sophisticated advances are common. Your specialist dealer should be abreast of these; otherwise the 'standard' cures already described should help; avoid making up 'cocktails' of various compounds – some may combine to produce toxic substances. Don't follow one treatment immediately with another – if successful, which ingredient worked?

7

BREEDING FISHES

TROPICAL

Some fish give birth direct to fully formed live baby fish; these are called ovoviviparous, usually shortened to viviparous. From them many interesting cross breeds, or hybrids, have been evolved. Others (oviparous) lay eggs in the normal way; these can be adhesive or not, scattered, carefully guarded in special sites and bubble nests, or even hatched in the parent fish's throat. The nests are all kinds, including floating air bubbles with the eggs individually wrapped in these hygienic containers.

The difficulty in breeding is so often not in the mating and spawning, but in the successful rearing of the fry, and this is one of the main reasons it is so much easier to breed the viviparous kinds, as the eggs are fertilised and hatched inside the mother's body and are thus virtually past the danger stage when born. Breeding problems vary from the extremely simple, say in the case of a livebearing Guppy, to the practically impossible in the case of the more rare egg layers like the Kuhli Loach. For this reason, detailed information is given under the descriptions of the individual fish at the end of this book, and the remarks here will deal with the general methods, applicable more or less to all occasions.

Where marine fishes are concerned, then things may not be too straightforward. In nature, many species only come together to breed, otherwise they follow an isolated existence. In these cases the actual courtship and spawning acts involve adult fishes requiring a large depth of water – something not likely to be available in the domestic aquarium. However, there is a growing list of modest-sized species which can be, and have been, bred in the aquarium. Such species follow the traditional egg-depositing methods as are found in freshwater cichlids, although the Seahorse has its own special method – it's the male who becomes pregnant! Just to make things even more confusing it is a regular occurrence amongst a group of marine fishes that sex reversal takes place, especially if something happens to the dominant male – a female will change sex to take his place as leader of the pack.

As previously stated, any information on captive breeding (if known) will be given under each individual species' description in a later chapter.

Breeding Tanks

The breeding tank is often quite shallow, perhaps 15–23cm deep, but it should not be too small – say, not less than 36cm long by 20cm high by 25cm wide – as many fish, such as the livebearing Molly, get nervous and excited when confined in small spaces and these nervous disorders can cause a disturbing number of complications. A large breeding tank is not necessary, although it is essential for the successful rearing of the young. This was one of the points mentioned in Chapter 1 as being vital for the future health of the babies; overcrowding is bad, in that all the fish are retarded in growth and strength; in fact Nature often takes a hand, causing a fatal epidemic and so destroying the weaker fish, leaving the others sufficient room for proper growth. For rearing, too, as distinct from breeding, the deepest tank – say, 30cm – is advantageous since it encourages the development of better specimens.

When plants are being used, the planted side of the breeding tank should always be towards the light, because that is the way the fry will instinctively turn in order to seek hiding places and protection.

Breeding Trap

In many instances a breeding trap is used inside the rearing tank, so as to separate the parents or parent from the eggs or live young. These traps are of many types – V-shaped, or a layer of glass rods spaced apart, perforated plastic sheeting, finely meshed plastic netting – all designed to allow eggs and live babies to drop through into the rearing tank beyond the reach of the adult who cannot pass through the same gap. Some livebearing females may give birth prematurely if placed in too small a trap; a well-planted nursery tank is better. As is well known, the parents so often eat the young fish or their eggs; where this does not apply, the breeding trap is quite unnecessary.

Choosing And Conditioning The Parents
The parents should be chosen with great care, the individual fish being the best obtainable, having regard to size, shape, colour, finnage, and so on; further, the prospective parents should like each other, that is, harmonise. The best way to ensure this is to place a group of adult fish in a tank and wait for them to 'pair off', the chosen ones being transferred to separate tanks.

With the egg layers, two or even more males are often used with one female. If the sexes are kept separately, brought to breeding condition as described below, and are then placed in the mating tank at night, they will often spawn next morning. Better still, if they can be put together at dawn, they will, in the morning, tend to spawn almost at once. It is usual to put the weaker fish (often the female) in first, so that it is already feeling at home before meeting the other fish.

Green water and/or two hours daily of sunlight are helpful in bringing the parents to breeding condition. Live foods, too, are practically essential: *Daphnia*, *Tubifex* worms, chopped earthworms, etc., can be given twice a day, enough at one feeding to last about 15–30 minutes. Too many white worms will tend to make the fish fat and reluctant to spawn. The rule is, therefore, to feed well but not too heavily.

As explained in the section on feeding, the frequency really depends on the water temperature: below 21°C for tropical fish their appetite is sluggish, at 24°C it is very keen, after 28°C the lowered oxygen content of the water reduces the appetite again. Similarly, for coldwater fish, the temperatures vary approximately from 10°C to 18°C and 22°C – approximately because various types of fish have varying optimum temperature ranges.

The temperature of the mating tank is often raised by 1–3°C when the adult fish are introduced, as this is bound to help spawning, and this higher temperature can be maintained until the eggs are hatched and even for the early stages of the fry. Restraint must be exercised, however, as explained in Chapter 1, lest the prolonged increase in temperature causes the fry to grow so fast as to be weakened. Once spawning is completed, the parents are separated from the eggs or young, except the cichlids, or, in the case of the labyrinth breathers, where the male only should be left with the nest for about a week. (Types of fish are described in a later part of the book.)

Types Of Eggs And Their Care
As has already been emphasised, different types of fish have varying preferences and methods of laying their eggs, but the following general remarks will serve as some guide.

1. Adhesive Eggs
Fish will often take care and trouble to choose the spot where these adhesive eggs will be laid. Broad leaves of a strongly growing plant like *Sagittaria* or *Cryptocoryne* are used; so too are the insides of small flower pots, or even the hollow of a conveniently shaped rock; some fish, of course, merely scatter their adhesive eggs which should be caught by bushy plants grouped in bunches.

2. Non-adhesive Eggs
These may be freely scattered, as for example on thickets of plants, noticeably those with fine leaves like *Myriophyllum*, *Ambulia*, *Cabomba*, or even Hair Grass (*Eleocharis*), which serve partly to catch the eggs but more especially to hide them, and the newly hatched fry, from the dangers of being eaten. Alternatively, the eggs are placed in carefully formed and guarded areas; especially is this so with the cichlids, which often use a hollow in the sand which they will guard against all comers. The same is true of the very interesting bubble-nest

builders, as detailed in the appropriate chapter.

How To Move The Eggs

In lifting out the plants which are holding the eggs, it is most unwise to subject them to sudden temperature changes or to expose them to the air. A simple plan is to place a bowl under these plants, raise the bowl (taking care to keep the plants, roots if any, and eggs submerged) and so to move them – still in their same water – to the rearing tank of the same temperature.

General questions such as whether the water should be 'old', green, or what its pH or DH should be, or whether the floor should be spotlessly clean or covered with some mulm, can only be answered in the case of particular breeding adult fish. They are mentioned here simply so that they can be noted by the hobbyist, helping him to overcome unexplained difficulties. The fry will need 'mature' water for their growth.

The same applies also to temperature and aeration, but it should be remembered, however, that fish accustomed to constant aeration will have to be taught gradually to do without it. Provided a tank is large enough, there should be no need for more than gentle aeration.

In all breeding routine, the question of cleanliness and the danger of infection will have to be watched most carefully. All nets, planting sticks, even the aquarist's hands, should be sterilised regularly.

Infertile Eggs, Hatching Problems

Eggs that prove infertile, often becoming covered with fungus, should be removed if possible and effort made to find out why they did not hatch in the normal way.

It is often found that some, or even many, eggs are covered with fungus but it is rare for all to be bad.

Snails eat eggs and should always be removed from the breeding tank but not necessarily from the rearing tank where they will help to keep the bottom clean – they will not eat the fry.

Should fertilised eggs not hatch, the causes may be:
1. Wrong temperature.

2. Too much or too little light. Some Tetras' eggs need a few days of darkness.
3. Dirt.
4. Polluted water due to feeding too soon; wait until fry have absorbed yolk sacs and swim freely before feeding.
5. Unsuitable water that might contain harmful gases or matter. Filter the tap water through filter floss or fine sand, and through activated charcoal, such as Hydraffin (bought from specialist dealers); or use rainwater instead. Perhaps the water was too deep.
6. Incorrect acidity/alkalinity of water, or of hardness/ softness. Check water pH and DH. If new water has been used, try 'seasoned' water, obtained by drawing from the tap and leaving in bright light (sunlight if possible) for a day; without disturbing the precipitate that will have formed at the bottom, siphon off the water into another clean container and leave it there (again in the sunlight if possible) to mature for a further 24–48 hours. The siphoning gets rid of any insoluble or floating matter.
7. Eggs not fertilised: perhaps the pair of adults did not harmonise – suggest the use of additional males, say two or three males to one female.
8. Tank too small.
9. Scum on top of the water, or cold draughts as you lift the tank cover, can wreak havoc.
10. Bacterial damage. Aureomycin sufficient just to tinge the water (or methylene blue), coupled with light aeration, should prevent this.

Further Hints On Breeding
If the water in the shallow breeding tank is too low to hold the heater unit comfortably, the latter can be immersed into a jar standing in the tank. Thus the water temperature of the tank will govern that of the water in the jar, so ensuring correct response by the thermostat.

In removing fry, it is advisable to use a fry-catcher, as netting may harm them. This is used in a scooping action, the fry being allowed to swim into the bowl.

Keep the water level of the rearing tank well below that of the tank sides as a protection against draughts. A glass cover is an additional protection against temperature fluctuations and dust – important at this fry stage.

Feeding

The mating and spawning process is often easier than the rearing of the fry. The most common difficulties are insufficient or unsuitable food at the early stages, and lack of space.

When the eggs are hatched, or the viviparous babies are born, in both instances a 'yolk sac' is attached to the fry with sufficient food for the initial period which may last from a few hours to two or three days, especially if supplemented by the addition to the tank of liberal quantities of green water, which is automatically rich in baby food. The yolk sac gone, the hobbyist must assume responsibility, especially for the egg-layed fry which are very tiny and need microscopic-sized food. Such food should be available *constantly* once the fish are swimming; and leaving a dim light on over the tank will encourage 24-hour feeding. Originally, infusoria cultures were the fishkeeper's only resort; these were infusions (hence the name) of vegetable matter – lettuce leaves, banana skins, sliced potatoes, hay – which were allowed to decay in some standing water. The resultant 'brew' teemed with microscopic life and was 'drip fed' into the aquarium. Unfortunately, such cultures were not always predictable in their results, they had to be renewed every few days, and sometimes all you got was a nasty smell!

Many fishkeepers develop their own patent starter foods – the yolk of a hard boiled egg, mashed *Daphnia*, shredded earthworms, all blended in a food processor can be tried – but the risk of polluting the water should not be overlooked.

Just as the dietary needs of adult fishes have been progressively researched and proprietary foods developed, so too have fry foods. Plankton (and infusoria) cultures are commonly available, as are liquidised foods – the latter in separate forms for egg-laying and livebearing species; finely powdered versions of flake foods can be taken by all but the smallest fishes.

Once the fry have trebled their size, they might be said to be past the difficult stage in their development, but they still have to be weaned onto the larger foods.

'Micro' has been introduced from Sweden, thanks largely to the kindness of Mrs Morten Grindal, of Solna; these minute worms are small enough to be fed to the fry at their present difficult stage. Alternatively, rotifers, newly hatched brine shrimps, dry powdered food, will all do and, at a slightly later stage, finely sifted *Daphnia*.

Watch with a magnifying glass – if the fry reject the food, it is still too big for them.

They should, however, be fed very frequently at this stage, say up to eight times a day, and a limited amount of sediment should be allowed to accumulate as it helps to grow the plants and infusoria. Of course, the danger of siphoning off fry as well as sediment is very real and will call for both patience and skill.

To repeat: all the remarks above are applicable only in the general sense; Neon Tetras, for example, like a spotlessly clean tank for their fry; and reference should be made to the end of the book for detailed points of advice. However, this chapter will serve as a general guide for the enthusiast who has persevered thus far.

COLDWATER

A controversial point should be mentioned at the start: should the breeding be done in a pond or in an aquarium?

The two really great advantages of the pond are its relatively large volume of water, and, in good weather, its abundance of natural foods for the young fish.

The disadvantages lie in the whims of the British climate; apart from extremes of heat or frost and ice, the normal temperature variations are very great indeed, 10°C being quite frequent, and there is little the average aquarist can do to control them. Furthermore, these changes are rapid, occurring within a few hours. So, too, is there a great discrepancy in the amount of light, especially sunlight, and an evenly spread supply is almost hopeless.

But these disadvantages have their attenuating factors. Although the atmospheric temperature changes very quickly, a fairly large volume of water is affected only slowly and cushions the fish from the worst of the shock. This is particularly so if the water is about a metre deep. Secondly, the fish seem to have a natural ability to pick out the coming fine weather and will normally spawn just at the start of a good spell; they cannot, of course, *make* good weather and the fine spells in Britain have a nasty tendency to fade off after a very few days.

Just as natural foods are abundant in open ponds, so too, on occasions, are fish lice and other waterborne enemies. The pond should, therefore, be capable of being thoroughly cleaned.

Naturally enough, no other fish, apart from the selected parents, must be present to spoil the quality of the spawnings. This also means that the pond should be periodically emptied to ensure that overlooked eggs or fry from previous matings have not remained behind to grow and to interbreed with the chosen parents.

If the aquarist has decided to do the breeding in ponds, he may still be well advised to hatch the eggs in an aquarium and to keep the fry indoors for the first crucial ten weeks. A pond that is more or less bare, except for ideal spawning plants at the shallow edge, practically forces the fish to spawn on these plants which can then easily be removed to an aquarium; fresh supplies of plants should be available to keep up with the spawnings.

It is important that these bunches of plants be frequently rinsed to shake off dead algae or any other such foreign matter that could later prevent the eggs from adhering properly.

If the parents are not separated from the eggs, many of these will be eaten. Even more important, once the fry have appeared, it is the slower swimming ones that get less of the food and are more subject to being attacked; the slower swimmers are usually those with the longer finnage – the very fish that the aquarist would most like to save.

Obviously, spawning starts with good quality parents that have been separately brought up to the best possible condition.

It is a bad mistake to use inferior fish as the resulting fry are just not worth the trouble. Each prospective parent should be known to have come from good stock and, even if not perfect in itself, be known to be capable of producing good young.

Sexing the fish is difficult. In Fancy Goldfish varieties, such as the Veiltail and the Fantail, the males are often as full bodied as the females. Only at breeding condition do the male tubercles appear as raised white dots on the gill plates and on the pectoral fins; an absence of these dots might mean that the fish is a female or that it is a male not ready to breed. Once spawning starts, however, the females can easily be picked out as they are vigorously chased and nuzzled by the males.

The breeding season normally begins at the end of April. Two or more males should be used to 'drive' each female in the well-known chase which may last a few hours or even two or three days. Thus, frequent replacements of plants, to catch the eggs as they are scattered, and plenty of swimming room are essential. In the aquarium a good supply of aeration helps. The water temperature should not be below 16°C or above 27°C; in the one, fish tend to be sluggish, in the other, they lack oxygen. 20–22°C is ideal for the driving, and bright light (especially sunlight) is appreciated.

The eggs, transparent, adhesive and the size of a pinhead, are laid in clusters, no two individual eggs being in contact. Within 24–48 hours the infertile ones turn opaque, almost milky; there always seem so many of these that the aquarist despairs of any hatching out, but patience and diligence are usually rewarded.

21–24°C is a good temperature for the incubation, and in four days fry should appear. They are free-swimming within 48 hours and will need green water, fry foods, etc., as described in detail in the section on feeding. Most of all, they will need plenty of space. Warmth, space and ample foods are all essential. As many as one thousand fry can result from a good spawning, so that the problem of space is pressing; it is most strongly advised to pick out the best specimens as soon as is practicable and to concentrate on them alone, disposing of the others. Aeration is helpful right from the commencement of the incubation period.

A temperature that is excessively high forces the growth of the fish and seriously weakens their constitution. It sometimes overdevelops the finnage too.

All along the line, inferior fish should be removed. For example, with Fantails, Veilteils and Moors, the ones with only single tails instead of the prized double tails can be detected well before they are fourteen days old and should be taken out. Later, as body shapes develop, the poor quality should be ruthlessly sacrificed. By the time three months have passed, the selection should have been completed.

Within two weeks, the fry are past the fry-food stage and will swallow finely powdered dry foods, dried eggs, oatmeal, etc. Great care must be taken not to foul the water, which can often be part changed, especially if snails are not able to cope with the work. Another few days, and the micro worms, finely sifted *Daphnia*, newly hatched brine shrimps fattened in green water, and not quite such powdered dry foods should be introduced. Within three to four weeks, the last stage of *Tubifex* and chopped white worms is reached. The worst danger is now over.

Meanwhile, the difficulty has been to get the fish to colour. The scales should be transparent so that a good body colour can be seen through them; often the scales remain opaque and a dark, uninteresting fish results.

If the parents have come from good stock, if the temperatures suggested above have been maintained, if ample space has been provided, if plenty of live foods were constantly given and if the Clerk of the Weather has kindly provided sunlight, then the fry should colour within eight months, some even within four months. A constant drip flow of water into the aquarium helps enormously. If a year goes by without the colour showing through, then hope of obtaining a good fish cannot be high.

It is sometimes suggested that the aquarium bottom painted a bright colour such as yellow or red influences the colour development of the fry, and there is some evidence of this. General conditions, including the surrounding colours and their interaction with sunlight, do influence the fry development and this suggestion should not be dismissed too lightly.

Fry born in May/June and reaching 8cm by the late autumn can usually winter out of doors for the hardier types such as Shubunkins and Fantails. August/September hatchings should be reared indoors. Veiltails, Moors and Lionheads are far better kept in aquaria. Once the fry have successfully survived one winter they are themselves ready to take an active part in this question of breeding; the best age, however, is some two years later when they have grown considerably.

The above descriptions apply to coldwater aquarium fish in general. It is remembered that strictly *pond* fish such as Goldfish, Koi, Carp, Rudd, Orfe, Tench, etc., are not being discussed, although their breeding conforms in the main with that detailed above.

In Chapter 9 are illustrated some of the best aquarium coldwater fish, together with some additional comments on them.

Conclusion

Breeding is not so much a matter of hard and fast rules as of 'feeling' and common sense; conditions, waters, fish, foods, sunlight and the like all vary from place to place and from time to time. Patience is essential, as periodical failures and disappointments are quite certain to occur.

Whilst the majority of breeding aquarium fishes follows a well-established pattern, it is in the breeding of marine species where the greatest challenges and perhaps the highest rewards (particularly in respect of conservation) still lay. There is still time for the aquarist to become a true pioneer.

8

PONDS

The following points will make a big difference to the pleasure of the owner and the health of the fish.

1. Today's ponds are not back-breaking affairs to install (once the hole has been dug) for they are more likely to be of rigid pre-formed fibreglass construction or else be lined with plastic or butyl rubber sheeting.

2. *Depth.* Either by sloping the floor or by building it in ledges, varying depths should be provided from 25–125cm. At 125cm the fish are pretty well protected from outside enemies and from changes of temperature, either excessive heat or cold. A further protection is to build at this depth a sort of 'home', i.e. a box open at one side into which they can retire in case of marauders – birds, cats or small boys. The shallow parts will be enjoyed by the fish on warm sunny days and should be furnished with marginal plants.

3. *Location.* Normal sunshine is most desirable but not to excess; all-the-day-long exposure to the sun is almost certain to turn the water green. On the other hand, a lack of shelter from east winds is not helpful. Dead leaves foul the water so that direct overhanging trees ought to be avoided. Excessive dirt and mud can be kept out of the pond if its edges are above the immediate ground level.

4. Facilities for emptying the pond either through a bottom drain or by means of a siphon to some lower level will be a great asset.

Treatment Of New Ponds

If built using concrete and cement, steps must be taken to prevent the pond water becoming contaminated by their lime content. Proprietary 'paint on' sealants will do the job easily, obviating the need to use chemicals such as potassium permanganate (which necessitated draining and refilling the pond once it had achieved its purpose), although some of the more garish, swimming-pool-blue colours should be avoided. As with the indoor aquarium, the pond should be left to its own devices for a week or two to stabilise itself before fish are introduced.

Plants

There are four main types of pond plant: border or marginal, that grow in 8–23cm of water; submerged oxygenators; lilies; and floating plants.

Instead of covering the base of the pond with earth, loam or even sand – all of which will tend to cloud the water – experience indicates that a better method is to plant bunches in specially designed, perforated plastic planting baskets and then immerse; they can be readily removed in case of need. Heavy loam, held down by a layer of medium-sized pebbles is the best planting medium, and it can be renewed from time to time, depending on the relative size of the roots and of the box.

There are many of these plants available – of lilies alone there are some 200 varieties – but the more popular ones are as follows: any specialist dealer will stock them.

Marginal. Often with flowers on which the insects will alight to lay their eggs and help provide natural foods for the fish.

Forget-me-nots
Arrowheads
Irises
Marsh Marigolds
Buttercups
Mint
Rushes
and Reeds

Submerged Oxygenators help to keep the water sweet. They

also provide a nursery where the eggs can hatch and the fry can grow in some degree of safety, and then feed on natural foods, such as infusoria, larva, louse, shrimps and *Daphnia*. Too many plants will choke a pond but fairly plentiful and thick bunches should be provided, leaving the fish enough room to swim freely.

The main submerged oxygenators are:

Elodea
Water Crowfoot
Starwort
Fontinalis
Hornwort
Myriophyllum

Lilies. The large, spreading leaves of the lily provide admirable shade for the fish and greatly encourage the development of natural insect life. Lilies are particular regarding the depth of water and their leaves will curl up if this is wrong or they are planted too near each other. Of the huge number of varieties available the Laydeckeri group favour 30–40cm water depth, and the Odorata 45–60cm depth. The use of special baskets is recommended for planting. Good sunlight is essential if they are to flower and flourish.

Floating Plants, i.e. those that are not rooted in anything but draw their nourishment either from the atmosphere or from the water; they are excellent for providing shade where needed. Naturally, since they float, there is no planting required in this case; all that is necessary is to put them in the water, preferably not upside down.

Pond Fish

As has already been stressed, these are in a different category from coldwater aquarium fish, being in the main quicker consumers of oxygen dissolved in the water; they are bigger for one thing, growing to over 45cm in length, and living for twenty to thirty years *or more*. They are often fast swimmers into the bargain, so that they burn up more energy and therefore need more oxygen. Although they have been kept in coldwater tanks it cannot be too strongly emphasised that it is not fair to the fish, which suffer a protracted agony of stunted growth and slow suffocation.

Goldfish, Silver Rudd, Golden Orfe, Nymphs, Comets, even Fantails, are all perfectly happy in ponds. The addition of scavengers – fish that grub around cleaning up the bottom – is advisable; notably Prussian and Golden Carp, Tench, but not Catfish which grow large and become very predatory. Koi are very popular (and voracious plant-eaters) requiring special pond conditions (large filtration systems for instance) outside the scope of this book.

River fish such as Pike or Perch are killers and must not be introduced; nor should Minnows, since they prefer fast-moving waters and are often carriers of disease.

Feeding

In summer time, particularly if the weather is good, the fish will find natural food in a well-planted pond; even so they could be given a small pinch of prepared food per fish twice a week. If, however, deliberate breeding is being attempted or the colour development of a fish is being forced, we refer the reader to Chapter 7 for instructions. From mid-September to mid-November serious attempts should be made purposely to fatten up the fish, so as to build up surplus fat and energy to enable them to survive the winter better. Once the water temperature falls below 10°C the fish become sluggish and do not eat; this winter hibernation lasts through until the warm weather of spring and no food should be given during the whole of this period.

The fattening-up process can be done by supplying a daily feed of worms, obtainable from a dealer or from compost heaps in the garden; in addition, there are special autumn-applicable foods available having a higher cereal (wheatgerm) content for this very purpose.

Of course, the dates stated in this chapter are approximate, being governed by the state of the weather and by the location and depth of the pond.

Preparing For The Winter

There are two main dangers, both equally important, especially in the case of the smaller ponds.

1. *Freezing.* Provided the pond is 125cm deep in one part at least, this battle is practically won so far as the normal British climate is concerned. When the top of the pond is coated with ice, it is a good plan to leave this unbroken except for two or four holes through which the air can circulate; then some 5cm of water can be siphoned off, leaving a protective air cushion in addition to the protective ice layer and so minimising the danger of any more of the pond water freezing. Snow 'blacks out' a pond and must be swept off the ice. The holes can best be made by standing a can of hot water on the ice until it melts; breaking with a hammer might stun the fish. Floating electric pond heaters will maintain an open space in any ice more easily.

2. *Foul Water.* This danger is often overlooked but it is very real. During the warm months the pond water content of gases and of minerals gradually increases, due to the decomposition of fish droppings, decaying leaves, and other such natural causes, until a high concentration is reached. In a frozen pond with its limited air openings, this high concentration can cause the water to go foul. Thus the following precautions are necessary in late November.

    (a) Cut back the growing submerged plants to within 15cm of the bottom, removing all excess.

    (b) Carefully remove as many dead leaves and as much foreign matter as is possible.

    (c) Change a third to half of the water gradually over 24–36 hours. If the frozen pond later seems to be going foul in spite of these precautions, then the risk of gradually changing a third to a half of the water in winter will have to be run.

Spring

This is the time fish may die as a result of the rigours of the winter, but there is little that can be done as the main remedies lie in attention during the previous November onwards to the points outlined above.

At this time, too, there is a particular danger of the water going green if the days happen to be bright; as the reader already knows, light promotes the growth of green microscopic life (algae), and since the plants have not yet started to grow and to compete for the even smaller living organisms that serve both algae and plants as food, the development of green algae is unhindered. Live *Daphnia* can be introduced into the pond and will soon eat up the algae, thus clearing the water; when the fish start eating as the spring warmth raises the pond water temperature, they will eat the *Daphnia* in their turn.

Water Cloudiness In Ponds

In the case of ponds, the remarks on water cloudiness in Chapter 4 apply, but in a slightly different form.

White cloudiness is very rare indeed and can more or less be ignored. Brown cloudiness is also less prevalent unless the pond is too shallow to allow floating matter to settle quickly, or unless large amounts of dirt, mud, dead leaves, and so forth, are at the bottom and are being stirred up by fish, particularly such fish as the Carp or Tench which love to burrow and grub along the bottom sediment.

Green cloudiness, however, is a common complaint in the bright days of summer. Try to shade about a third of the pond surface – floating plants, or lilies with spreading leaves are helpful. Also, strongly growing submerged plants hinder the development of algae. It is generally accepted that the most efficient method of clearing green water is to use ultra-violet light in conjunction with the pond's filtration system; the UV light coagulates the unicellular algae into sufficiently large globules which can then be removed by the filter medium. However, this method doesn't help with 'blanketweed' – that is, the long blue-green strips and even webs that entwine and suffocate plants.

There are various ways of dealing with this horrible weed: regularly removing it, physically, with a twisted stick, as and when it appears; using algicides to kill it off – but the dead materials then have to be removed and there is no guarantee that a passing frog might not reinfect the pond with a small piece stuck to its back! One of the most recent proprietary remedies specifically produced to deal with this pest actually alters the water composition to deny blanketweed the necessary nutrients to grow; it is a course of treatment which lasts three weeks, with repeated doses periodically required. Other methods include changing the water's composition by electronic means or by magnetism; a less sophisticated method entails simply removing phosphates from the water as these form a necessary part of blanketweed's nutritional requirements.

General Facts

The gallon capacity of a pond can be determined by multiplying in feet the length by the width by the depth by $6\frac{1}{4}$. The capacity in litres is the product of length by the depth by the width in centimetres, divided by 1000.

For a circular pond, multiply in feet the diameter by the diameter by the depth by 4.9 to get the number of gallons. For litres, multiply half the diameter by half the diameter by the depth (all in centimetres) by 3.14 and divide by 1000.

The number of fish that can be kept is one body inch of fish per square foot of water surface. Thus a 10 ft by 3 ft pond (30 square foot) will hold ten fish 3 inches long, not counting finnage. Measuring metrically, you can say that 1cm of fish needs 365 square cm of water surface area. Thus a pond of 3m by 1m could hold around ten fish, each 8cm long.

Spawning, rearing and water enemies have been dealt with elsewhere.

Fountain pumps have the same effect as aeration – detailed in Chapter 3.

Rocks should not be used for the simple reason that they cannot easily be seen; their purpose is decorative, so as they are not visible, why use them? A rockery round the edge is quite a different matter.

Rigid ponds, made of plastic compounds, can be plonked literally on your sitting room carpet to make a most pleasing indoor pond. Increasingly popular are the indoor ponds raised on decorative stands (often incorporating flowers/speciality lighting) to bring the pond up to standing or to sitting level – so that you can talk to the fish, tickle them, cup them in your hand (immersed in the water), and generally tame these lovable pets.

Add a small fountain and/or a waterfall cascade and you also have the therapeutic, soothing sound of gently falling water – marvellous for relaxation.

Add a heating unit; combine it with exotic plants, partly submerged, partly surface, partly growing up into your room; have the full range of tropical fish available; and you'll wonder why you never had it before.

9

COLDWATER FISH FOR THE AQUARIUM

Shubunkin
The hardiest of all coldwater fish. Although treated here as an aquarium variety of Goldfish, it can live outdoors throughout the year. Average life fourteen years. Our illustration shows an excellent specimen, both as regards body shape and finnage. The covering scales should be quite transparent, showing a beautiful assortment of mottled colours; blue should predominate over smudges of red, brown, yellow and violet with a peppering of black flecks. There are two main types of

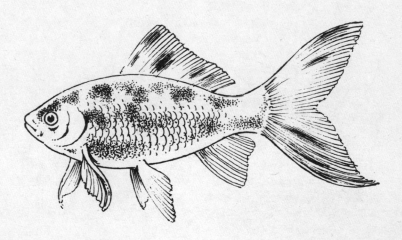

Fig. 6 Shubunkin

Shubunkin, the London and the Bristol; of these, the London has the slimmer body and the shorter tail. The Bristol is noted for the large, rounded lobes of the tail fin.

At 16°C to 21°C it spawns readily, the eggs hatching in four days. Four spawnings a season (April to September) is ample.

Fantail

Our illustration clearly shows the best type of egg-shaped body and finnage, together with their relative proportions; note that the tail and partially hidden anal fin are 'double' unlike the 'single' tail of the Shubunkin. Like the Shubunkin, the Fantail is an all-year-round pond fish and has a maximum life of around thirteen years.

This fish will breed after surviving one winter, but it is better to be developed for another year or so before breeding. It is still lively at the age of ten years and is a hardy pet which takes most foods and can live out of doors throughout the year.

Born a dark greenish brown, the best specimens develop in four to eight months into a warm gold.

Fig. 7 Fantail

Veiltail

Our illustration clearly shows the rounded body, as distinct from the egg-shaped one of the Fantail, and the different finnage especially in the entire absence of a fork in the less stiffly held, trailing caudal fin which, again, is 'double'.

Fig. 8 Veiltail

Telescopic-eyed Moor

Jet-black, double tailed and telescopic-eyed – those are its characteristics. Very short sighted and best kept in the aquarium. A fish which requires careful feeding, including

Fig. 9 Telescopic-eyed Moor

algae. A good plan is to drop the food in the same place each time, calling the fish by tapping gently on the glass. Dislikes cold and should not be below 10°C, preferring 18–21°C. Good light, but not bright sunlight, is appreciated.

Lionhead
The body is that of a Veiltail, with the finnage of a Fantail. The pimply head growth gives it its distinctive appearance and name and takes four to six years to develop. Has no dorsal fin. Likes aeration to help in its breathing, which is rather laborious due to its tremendous growth on the head. Can easily be killed by the water becoming foul or otherwise running out of oxygen.

Oranda
Very similar to the Lionhead, except that the growth of its mane is not so pronounced; a distinctive dorsal fin and more flowing finnage compensates for this.

Fig. 10 Lionhead

Other Varieties

The Celestial, Bubble Eye and Pom Pon are three more long-established Fancy Goldfish strains, but in recent years the number of direct importations from the Far East, featuring such delights as Chocolate and Sunset Orandas, Blue Ranchus and Lilac Velvet Dragon Eyes, has increased dramatically. Finally, do not overlook some of the colourful Bitterlings (*Rhodeus* spp) or some of the now commonly available North American native fishes such as the Red Shiner (*Cyprinella* sp) and Sunfishes (*Lepomis* spp).

Licences

Recent government legislation in the UK requires licences to be held by both vendor and purchaser with regard to selling, buying and owning certain coldwater fishes.

10

TROPICAL FISH FOR THE AQUARIUM: LIVEBEARERS

As is well known, there are fish that do not lay eggs but give direct birth to live baby fish, miniature creatures about 0.5cm long but fully formed and able to swim at once. The eggs are fertilised and developed inside the mother; during the period of gestation they are kept folded in half, head to tail. The length of the gestation depends on the aquarium conditions, but principally on the temperature, which should not be too low.

In livebearers the sexes are easily distinguished. The male anal fin quickly develops into a pointed instrument known as the gonopodium; normally carried at rest parallel to the body and pointing backwards, it is brought right forward for use when the act of fertilisation is imminent. The female anal fin is rounded.

The males are promiscuous and have no interest whatsoever in caring for their young. Curiously enough, a single fertilisation can result in several subsequent spawnings by the female without any further contact, the spawnings each being separated by as many days (usually thirty or so) as the original period of gestation. However, this characteristic does not apply to all livebearing fishes only to what might be termed the 'cultivated' species such as Platies, Swordtails, Guppies and Mollies. Other more 'wild' genera, such as *Goodea*, *Ameca* and *Dermogenys,* for instance, require a mating for each brood.

After fertilisation the female gradually begins to swell, and her gravid spot, which is close to the vent, becomes darker and darker, and more and more intense in colour as the time for delivery approaches, when anything from half a dozen to fifty or even a hundred young are born. These are just over 0.5cm or more in length, and can swim at once, otherwise they would not escape the cannibalistic tendencies of their mother, who should be separated from them by breeding traps or some other device. The simplest device is to use massed plants, including floating *Riccia*; the fry have a natural instinct to swim towards the light and the protective thickets should be arranged accordingly. Well-fed adults do not make serious attempts to seek out the young.

Most of these viviparous fry are already past the fry food stage at birth and, accordingly, at warm temperatures of 24–27°C develop rapidly, *provided* they have plenty of room. Frequent feeding, even four to eight times daily, is advisable; the surplus food is eaten by snails or by *Corydoras* fish specially introduced to scavenge.

Guppy

The Guppy, scientific name *Poecilia reticulata*, is by far the most famous and the most easily bred of all the livebearers. Maximum length is 6cm for the female and just over 3cm for the male, not including the tail.

No two males are alike, although selective breeding can so fix major characteristics that there are numerous recognised sub-divisions, such as the Lyretail, Swordtail, etc., apart from the distinctive Golden Guppy.

Fig. 11 Guppy

The Guppy really has everything: lovely colourings (in the males only), hardy, active, playful, but extremely peaceful; stands temperatures from 16–38°C, eats anything, even lives in foul water and seldom falls sick. Our illustration shows various types of coloured males and one gravid female with her dark 'gravid' spot clearly visible.

At 22–27°C the period of gestation is only four weeks, but below temperatures of 20°C it is prolonged to nearly twelve weeks. At 26°C the fry, which can number from six to fifty, will grow so rapidly that they will be ripe for reproduction after as little as six weeks! Frequent feeding is almost essential. After two weeks a Guppy is definitely old.

Molly

There are five main kinds, all having a body shape not unlike a female Swordtail, and all vegetarian by preference.

Poecilia sphenops is the most often encountered. Growing up to 10cm in length, it is born silvery, becomes speckled with black and, in rare cases, finishes a pitch-velvet-black; usually the body remains spangled with an attractive blue/gold sheen. The males sometimes have an orange-tipped tail.

Terribly greedy, it eats practically all the time and is liable to overfeed; it loves green algae, or failing that, boiled spinach. Bright sunny locations, a clean tank, old water and temperatures of 24–27°C suit it well. As Mollies come from waters which may often be subjected to an occasional influx of salt water, the addition of a teaspoonful of rock salt per gallon of water can prove beneficial. A lively fish, it is peaceful to the point of being easily frightened, and is therefore liable to nervous diseases. It should not be netted or disturbed more than is necessary.

A gravid female becomes flustered and agitated in a confined breeding trap; in any case, she should never be disturbed when the delivery time of her young is less than two weeks away. A bang of a room door or sudden movements will frighten her, so that shade and privacy are practically essential.

They are seasonal breeders, so the aquarist should aim to have a virgin female some nine months old in breeding condition in April. At 24–27°C her first spawning will be ready in eight weeks, and the subsequent three spawnings at approximately thirty to thirty-five day intervals after this first one. Then the female should be rested until next year. The young can number anything from six to forty, and are nearly 1.25cm long at birth.

The best fish do not develop their sex characteristics before nine months. First the anal fin ceases to grow, then it loses its rounded trailing edge and becomes narrow and pointed. It shrinks, becomes narrower still, shows signs of detachment and finally becomes pointed. Then the gonopodium starts to grow. The chest of the male is far more square and wide.

The Molly is different from other livebearers in regard to the degree of nervousness and of the importance played by the seasons in breeding.

The largest Mollies, *Poecilia latipinna* and the similar *Poecilia velifera*, are both famed for their magnificent sail-like dorsal fins. In addition to the natural (wild) iridescent green forms, golden and albion aquarium-bred forms have been cultivated.

Black Molly, *Poecilia mexicana*. Born black and stays black; the trouble is that it never grows large.

Liberty Molly, whose body remains an uninteresting silver but whose dorsal is tricoloured, by way of compensation.

All these, and the others not mentioned, are being cross-bred to give lovely new varieties including Lyretail forms.

Swordtail

The Swordtail, scientific name *Xiphophorus hellerii*, has a maximum length (excluding the male tail sword) of 8cm. They have a distinct preference for variety in their diet but will take anything, not forgetting algae or boiled spinach. A temperature of 23°C is ideal. Most types of water will do, but a mature, clean tank is probably best.

In thickly planted tanks, which include floating plants, the parents are not too liable to eat the young, especially if plenty of other food is available. Breeding temperature is 23–27°C.

This Green Swordtail (and its more famous derivative the Red Swordtail) is a great jumper; the males have a tendency to fight among themselves, especially if insufficient females are present. It is very liable to develop 'shimmies' after even a

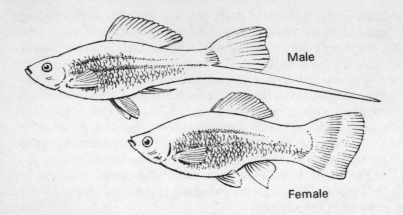

Fig. 12 Swordtail

single chilling, and should be kept at 23–27°C.

The best males do not grow their swords until they are some eight to ten months old and reach about 5cm in length; once the sword has started to appear, the fish does not grow much more. Likes plenty of light and can spawn up to two hundred young.

Whilst the wild Swordtail is green, many aquarium varieties have been bred including the Red-eyed Red, the Black, the Tuxedo, the Wagtail (black fins and mouth, single-coloured body), Double Sword, Lyretail Pineapple and Hi Fin. Sex reversal (female to male) is not uncommon.

Platy

The Platy, scientific name *Xiphophorus maculatus*, is another favourite livebearer, contributing a great number of similarly patterned hybrids to its relative the Swordtail. The male length is 4cm and the female 6cm. The main recognised sub-divisions are as follows:

Black Platy, so called because of the dominating bank of black that runs lengthwise from head to tail. The fringes of the body are tinged with green or yellow, and the fins are often white.

Golden Platy, with a rich yellow body, often has a red dorsal fin.

Fig. 13 Platy

Moon Platy, whose distinctive feature is a crescent-shaped half moon in the tail.

Red Platy, beautifully blood-red, is not quite as hardy as the others. The colour becomes deeper with age.

Wagtail Platy whose tail can almost be imagined to wag the body. The dorsal and ventral fins are well developed too; the fin colouring is usually black.

From the above half-dozen kinds, there have been very numerous crosses; it should be remembered that they are all Platies and will interbreed without any heed to colour or markings.

Xiphophorus variatus is a more slender species whose aquarium-developed forms include the Sunset and Marigold varieties.

Regardless of variety, Platies share the same dietary and aquarium requirements as their close relative the Swordtail.

In thickly planted tanks which include floating plants, the parents are not too liable to eat the young, especially if plenty of other food is available. Breeding temperature is 23–27°C.

11

TROPICAL FISH FOR THE AQUARIUM: EGG LAYERS

CYPRINIDS

Rosy Barb
Scientific name *Barbus conchonius*. Maximum length 9cm.

There are very many varieties of Barbs obtainable nowadays and they are lively and attractive additions to the community tank.

The Rosy Barb, like all its cousins, is hardy, playful to the point of being boisterous, always hungry and willing to eat

Fig. 14 Rosy Barb

practically any type of food, long lived (up to eight years), thriving best in old water and in bright locations. Temperature preference 23–26°C.

The male dorsal fin is black at its leading edge, while that of the female is almost colourless. Both have a black spot on the tail. At breeding condition the female is greenish gold and full bodied; her mate is a bright rosy red.

Spawning is fairly easy and lasts about two hours. Temperature 27°C. Plenty of space for the driving of the female by the male is required, as are thickets of *Cabomba* and *Myriophyllum* to catch the practically non-adhesive eggs – as described in the breeding of Zebra Danios. The water can be 20–30cm deep.

The eggs hatch in two days at 27°C and the fry are hardy; in fact, the main problem is to find enough room for the possible three hundred arrivals!

Tiger Barb
Scientific name *Barbus tetrazona* (formerly *Barbus sumatranus*). Maximum length 5cm.

Another of the more popular Barbs, it has a colourful red and black appearance, especially at temperatures above 24°C.

Fig. 15 Tiger Barb

Extremely lively, smaller specimens are better for the community tank.

The red in the ventral fins is more pronounced in the male; the female is fuller bodied.

Temperature and spawning are as described for the Rosy Barb. Needs a lively playmate and is best kept in sufficient numbers to prevent them from nipping other fishes' fins out of boredom.

Other Barbs

There are more than thirty types available, including many firm favourites:

ARULIUS BARB (*Barbus arulius*). Rather longer and thinner than the others, growing to 10cm and displaying pronounced black markings.

CHECKER BARB (*Barbus oligolepis*). Small and peaceful with varied checkered markings.

CHERRY BARB (*Barbus titteya*). Peaceful, almost shy. Lovely colours during breeding condition. Small.

GOLDEN DWARF BARB (*Barbus gelius*). Dwarf variety, and comparatively rare.

SIX BANDED BARB (*Barbus hexazona*). Long, sleek, colourful and well behaved.

TICTO BARB (*Barbus ticto*). Similar to the Rosy but with a more striking top fin, and with a luminous spot on the tail.

Harlequin

Scientific name *Rasbora heteromorpha*. Maximum length 4cm.

A delightful fish that has always been a favourite of the community aquarium. A striking black triangle dominates the rear half of the body, the fringes of which are tinged with red.

Peaceful and hardy, the Harlequin is at home in any temperature from 21–23°C, but prefers 25–28°C. It will eat almost any type of food. Usually swims about 15cm from the water surface, likes new water, slightly acid and softened to DH 6–8, and benefits from aeration.

Breeding is not too difficult, and the following may help: heavy clumps of strong growing *Cryptocorynes* at one end of the tank with the substrate sloping high up from the back right

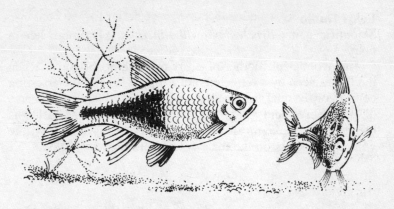

Fig. 16 Harlequin

down low to the front; new water that has been standing in strong light, preferably sunlight, for two days; pH 6.2 obtained by the use of rotting leaves rather than by sodium acid phosphate; dimmed light; gently dripping water at the planted end; temperature 25–28°C; clean tank, free from sediment; a very small amount of iron in the water, say, 1.5 parts per million; two males to one female; and DH 6–8.

Spawning first starts when the female swims upside down under selected leaves, rubbing herself against them, the male being in excited attendance. When he joins her under the leaf in a trembling embrace, the adhesive eggs are produced, fertilised and are stuck on to the leaf. The action lasts for about ninety minutes, with rests, and several leaves are used. As has already been suggested, the tank should be clean as algae covering the plants prevents the eggs adhering properly and fallen ones are soon eaten. Parents should be removed as soon as is practical. Fifty eggs is quite a satisfactory result; at 28°C they hatch in one day.

Pearl Danio

Scientific name *Brachydanio albolineatus*. Maximum length 6cm.

The wonderful mother-of-pearl hues shine brightest when the fish is seen by a reflected, not a top, light, and the arresting colours of the anal fin are then seen to best advantage. Gleams of purple, red and gold, and the flashing row of pearl dots brighten the make-up of this fish. At breeding condition the white body spots on the male colour into brownish pink.

Fig. 17 Pearl Danio

Peaceful, extremely lively, it is similar in habits and in breeding to its cousin the Zebra. The ways of sex differentiation are the same.

Zebra Danio

Scientific name *Brachydanio rerio*. Maximum length 4cm.

A delightful fish, fast swimming, playful and active but not mischievous, looks best in schools when the blue-black horizontal stripes on the pale background flash in the light. The background fluctuates through white to silver or even to yellow, depending on the lighting and on the surroundings; the darker the bottom of the aquarium, the darker the colours on the fish.

With a very wide temperature range it does best in 23–24°C. Has a comparatively short life span of three years

Fig. 18 Zebra Danio

and high temperatures tend to shorten this even more. Keeps near the surface and prefers to eat there; it will take almost any kind of food.

The sexes are easy to identify. The female is more full bodied, and is more arched than the male between the back of the head and the dorsal fin. In our illustration the top fish is the male.

In spawning, the main problem is to prevent the eggs being eaten. There are special breeding traps that allow the eggs to fall through but which prevent the parents following, or a layer of coarse pebbles and a breeding depth of 10cm of water can be used, the eggs falling fast and being protected by the crevices between the pebbles. Brought up to condition separately, the female should first be introduced into the breeding tank, the male the same evening, and the spawning can be expected next morning at first light if the temperature is raised from 22–23°C to 26°C. At first the female chases the male, but the roles are soon reversed.

About one hundred eggs are given out in excited bursts, and are fertilised by the male; the action taking place right close to the top of the water – almost out of it at times. If he is in poor condition, or if the eggs have been too scattered, a high proportion of infertile ones can result; the rest hatching in two or three days at 26°C. The parents should be removed after spawning. Neutral water of pH 7.0, not too old, is best. Groups of plants in which the males can corner the females and urge them to lay are advisable.

White Cloud Mountain Minnow

Scientific name *Tanichthys albonubes*. Maximum length 4cm.

When young it looks just like a Neon Tetra with the luminous bright green streak, but this gradually fades as adult size is reached and becomes greenish-yellow. As a compensation the red colour develops in the fins. Incidentally, it is in these fins that is seen most clearly the difference between the two distinct strains that are said to exist.

Peaceful and hardy, the fish has an amazing temperature range from 7°C to some 32°C, but should normally be kept round 22°C. In common with most small-mouthed fish, it prefers frequent feeding, say, three times daily, and likes soft, new water of pH 6.8.

The male, being more colourful and slimmer bodied than the female, also has a longer dorsal. The breeding habits are the same as that for the Zebra, with the non-adhesive eggs hatching in 72 hours at 22°C. Because the spawning action lasts for a week or so, the best results are probably obtained by separating the adults from the eggs by means of glass rods, plastic mesh or any other such device. Unlike the Zebra, these fish are not so prone to eat the eggs.

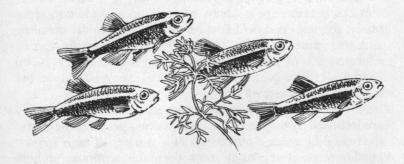

Fig. 19 White Cloud Mountain Minnow

CHARACINS

Glowlight Tetra
Scientific name is not known for certain but is currently accepted as *Hemigrammus erythrozonus*. Maximum length 4cm.

Beautiful is the only word to describe the shining eyes and the phosphorescent, warm-glowing streak running the length of the body. No black and white illustration can do it justice.

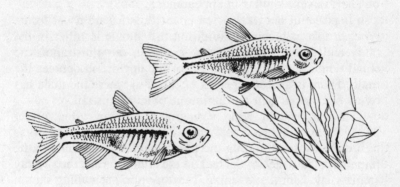

Fig. 20 Glowlight Tetra

It is best kept in groups of four or more. Peaceful and hardy, it is not finicky about food, although being a small eater prefers frequent meals. It likes a high oxygen and a low carbon dioxide content in its water, which should not be too old and which can profitably be aerated. The aquarium should be clean and kept at 23–24°C.

The breeding tank should be most carefully sterilised, be in dim light, be about 13–18cm deep and be kept at 27°C. Aeration helps. Spawning action is energetic, usually at water surface, and is over in thirty to forty minutes; the fish momentarily locking fins and rolling over on to their sides. Eggs are fertilised during the embrace, and a dozen or so are produced at a time. They are semi-adhesive and clumps of *Myriophyllum* or *Cabomba* make ideal spawning ground;

about 36 hours are enough to hatch the eggs.

This fish is subject to the 'Neon Tetra Disease' (a description of which is in that section) and fry should be kept in darkness for the first five days after hatching.

Beacon Fish

Scientific name *Hemigrammus ocellifer*, sometimes known as Head-and-Tail Light Fish, from its two luminous spots. Grows to nearly 5cm in length. The Pretty Tetra, *Hemigrammus pulcher*, is very similar in appearance.

It is peaceful but lively. Sex characteristics are usual for its type, in that at breeding condition the female is fuller in the body and is very liable to hen-peck. In our illustration the small white fleck in the anal fin of the upper fish denotes the male. There is another species of this fish where the male has two white flecks near the luminous point on his tail.

The fish have a wide temperature tolerance but prefer 23–24°C and will breed best at 23–26°C. As usual, spawning is best done by conditioning the pair separately, introducing the female first into the nuptial tank in the afternoon and the slightly scared male later that evening. Next morning spawning should commence, and will last up to 4–5 hours. If the male is being too hen-pecked, the operations should be postponed until he is in better condition. Mature water, sufficient for a depth of

Fig. 21 Beacon Fish

10–15cm, and the bushy clumps of *Myriophyllum* and *Cabomba* should be provided for the semi-adhesive eggs which hatch in 24 hours at 26–28°C. The addition of floating plants will help. The bottom of the breeding tank should be clear, and not be littered with pebbles or small stones.

Black Widow

Scientific name *Gymnocorymbus ternetzi*; it grows to 5cm but is at its best at 3–4cm; afterwards it becomes pale and loses the wonderful black markings from which it gets its name.

The caudal fin is transparent and hardly noticeable; the dorsal and anal fins and the rear half of the body are black; and the silver front half of the body is marked by three black bands. Our illustration does not quite bring out the peculiar disc-like shape.

It is a lively fish, but quite peaceful. Sex differences are not apparent, except that the female at breeding condition is fuller in body and considerably more assertive than the male. If a strong light is shone through the body, the female intestine will be seen to be more rounded, the male one slightly angular.

Tolerating a wide temperature range, it breeds at 26–27°C. Love play begins with the female driving the male from end to end of the tank until he is goaded into action. In spawning, the

Fig. 22 Black Widow

male repeatedly brushes the ventral of the female, tilting slightly as he touches her; the movements are rapid, but the eggs can be seen to fall. Some 150 eggs are laid in batches of a dozen or so.

At 27°C the adhesive eggs hatch in 12–24 hours, and the fry become free-swimming in four days.

Cardinal and Neon Tetras

At first glance, the slightly larger Cardinal, *Paracheirodon axelrodi*, might be mistaken for a Neon Tetra but look closely – the brilliant carmine red area covers the whole lower half of the body; that of the Neon stops halfway along, but both fishes still share the electric blue/green line topping the red. Needless to say, a tank containing a shoal of these fishes is almost indescribably beautiful.

The Neon Tetra, *Paracheirodon innesi*, grows to 4cm.

Surely all hobbyists have heard of this most dazzling aquarium fish. Our illustration simply does not do it justice, as no illustration, not even one in colour, could do that. Running lengthwise is a brilliant blue/green streak and immediately

Fig. 23 Cardinal and Neon Tetras

underneath another one of a bright red. Both lines seem luminous, and the effect is startling. Hardy and peaceful, the Neon will eat most foods, although its mouth is small, too small sometimes even to take *Daphnia*.

It prefers temperatures of 22–24°C and likes shade and privacy. The only sure way to tell the sexes is to wait for two adults of a group to pair off, the female being more full bodied.

Breeding the Neon has long been a challenge but the difficulties are now overcome with most Neons in the trade coming from Far East fish farms rather than their native South American rivers. Firstly, the parents must be healthy and free of the 'Neon Tetra' disease *Plistophora*; of this there are no external or visible marks, although the muscle tissues are sometimes slightly whitish. Infested fish lose weight and persistently lay infertile eggs. The disease is incurable; a parasite, protozoan, infects the intestines and the spore formation. Thus the presence of even one 'carrier fish' (i.e. one that is infected, but not virulently) can poison the water so that eggs do not hatch. Very great numbers of fish are so infected although they appear quite healthy and live for a long time. Aureomycin or methylene blue can help, in light doses sufficient just to tinge the water.

The main difficulty, then, is to get healthy parents. Furthermore, they must harmonise and have been brought up separately to breeding condition. Soft water, three days old, 12–70cm deep, pH 7.0 to 7.2, temperature 22–23°C, clumps of *Myriophyllum*, and absolute cleanliness make up the breeding tank. *Absolute* cleanliness is vital and everything will have to be most thoroughly scalded and sterilised; in fact, there are some breeders that just do not believe this can be sufficiently well done and insist on a bare, all-glass tank, with one propped-up flat stone to whose underneath the fry can later cling. Very dim lighting is also important, and, as soon as the normal spawning has taken place, the hatching aquarium should be kept in continuous darkness for five to six days. Furthermore, the water depth can be reduced to 6cm. Both these two unusual precautions seem to increase the proportion of fertile eggs. Hatching the eggs, not laying them, is the real trouble; some two hundred can be laid and are practically non-adhesive.

The fry are small, even when compared with other types of fry, and the greatest care in feeding is required. At 23–26°C the eggs should hatch in 24 hours and the alevin become free-swimming in four days. Remember, though, that continuous darkness is essential at this stage and that no direct light must be admitted to the tank, so that there is no means of examining the fry before the sixth day after spawning. Thereafter the light can be gradually returned to normal, but strong lights are to be avoided.

Flame Fish

Scientific name *Hyphessobrycon flammeus*. Maximum length 4cm.

A beautiful little fish, not flamboyant in colour but whose red flush is warm, especially on the tail half of the body. Peaceful and hardy, it has a preference for a bright, well-painted tank, free from dirt. It has a very wide temperature range and an average life of four years.

The anal fin in the male is pointed and is fitted with a small hook on the end; the hook is invisible to the eye but often gets caught in the fine meshing of a net. The outline of the female is not so straight as that of her partner, in fact it is more nearly concave. A strong light shone through the fish shows the

Fig. 24 Flame Fish

female intestines to be more rounded than the slightly angular ones of the male.

24–27°C is a good breeding temperature. Plenty of *Cabomba*, *Myriophyllum*, or other such plants, old water, slight aeration and two males to one female make up the ideal breeding combination. The male drives the female vigorously before they take up a side by side position, trembling violently and releasing the eggs in batches of a dozen every few minutes. A hundred eggs constitute a reasonable spawning. Obviously the parents should be removed before they can eat the eggs.

At 24–27°C these will hatch in some sixty hours and the fry become free-swimming in about four days.

Glass Tetra

Scientific name *Moenkhausia oligolepis*. Included here because it looks similar to the Beacon, although it belongs to a different group. Its luminous spots are more definitive. Decorative and peaceful. A further, smaller, species, *Moenkhausia sanctaefilomenae*, is also available.

Hatchet Fish

Scientific genus name *Carnegiella* species.

Both the Silver Winged and the Marble types are shaped like an inverted half moon with a flattened back. Top swimmers. Hardy. As these fish leap out of the water to catch their food in nature, keep the tank well covered – they jump when startled too!

X-Ray Fish

Scientific name *Pristella maxillaris*. Length only 4–4.5cm.

Its popularity is long established as a peaceful and lively foil for more brightly coloured fish. The stark contrast of its black markings on a white body is completed by a faintly pink tail.

The dark mark on the anal fin of the female goes right across; on the male it appears as a patch with a clear strip at both ends. At breeding condition the female is somewhat more full-bodied.

Bred in mature water of 18cm depth, the fish likes a tank planted with bushy *Myriophyllum* and *Cabomba*, especially

Fig. 25 X-Ray Fish

towards the lighted end; temperature should be 23–25°C, at which the eggs will hatch in a day. During spawnings, the parents indulge in energetic driving and finally end up side by side, quivering violently, fertilising the adhesive eggs which are laid on the vegetation.

CICHLIDS

Angel Fish
Scientific name *Pterophyllum scalare*. Maximum length 13cm.

'The queen of the aquarium' – certainly its distinctive shape, its quietly effective black markings on the silver body, and its dignified movement, especially in a group, can earn it the adjective 'royal'.

Happiest when in the company of other Angel Fish, this lovely creature should not be kept alone. An asset to any community tank, the Angel is inclined to be a little shy and might need to be fed separately; indeed, it is a little finicky in its food preference and is liable to go on hunger strikes. Live foods, above all *Daphnia*, are well received. Normal temperatures of 23–25°C are best.

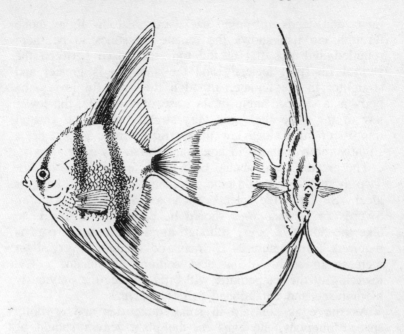

Fig. 26 Angel Fish

The real secret of keeping Angels is in the soft (DH 4) aquarium water. If this is not suitable, the fish does not thrive, and positively refuses to breed; even if it has bred, the eggs prove infertile and do not hatch.

The prospective parents should be allowed to choose themselves by your putting a group of fish together and allowing them to pair off, otherwise they will not harmonise. The preliminary courting is more like quarrelling in its violence, and has been known to end in death unless the fish are separated for a while before being reintroduced. Because harmony is essential the vexed question of determining the sex can better be left to the fish themselves, although two female Angels have been known to pair off to produce infertile eggs!

The following points will help to sex an adult fish. The female tube for depositing eggs is more rounded than the male and tends to point backwards; strong light shone through the fish shows the female intestines to be more rounded and less flat at the top; the space between the ventral fin (the 'feelers') and the anal fin is greater and straighter in the female, although the anal fin leaves the body at a sharper angle in the case of the male; the lower jaw of the male sticks out very slightly more; the general impression in a side view of the male frame is that he is slightly more rounded in appearance than his mate.

The breeding tank should be crystal clear and free of dirt. Two hours' direct sunshine coupled with some shade is ideal. Strong-leafed plants such as *Sagittaria*, Amazon Swords or *Crytocorynes* should be plentifully available to take the adhesive eggs, although ample swimming room is required. Temperature 24°C. Increased aeration, a very slight increase in acidity using acid sodium phosphate, a 1°C lowering of the temperature will often induce the previously harmonised and conditioned pair to spawn.

As the eggs are laid in small quantities and at fairly spaced intervals, the eggs on the plant leaves should be removed to water of exactly the same type and temperature. 8–10cm depth is enough. Gentle aeration is extremely helpful. If this constant removal of the eggs proves too costly in plants, strips of slate 5cm wide could be used instead, especially as these will not rot (like the leaves) during the comparatively long hatching period. Infertile eggs should be removed as they tend to swamp the others.

At 26–27°C the eggs hatch in about 48 hours, the fry being free-swimming in five to six days, although not reaching recognisable shape for some four weeks. The fry need plenty of oxygen, and aeration helps, as does soft water.

Also Available

Lace Angels, Veiltail Angels, Black Angels, Marble Angels, Blushing Angels, Bicolor Angels and many others. Despite being a South American species by nature, most Angel Fish sold today are captive-bred, originating in fish farms in the Far East.

Discus

Almost completely circular, with wonderful markings when grown to its full size of 30cm diameter. Expensive but highly prized. Apart from the original species, *Symphysodon discus*, there are many colour hybrids, aquarium-developed from the ever popular *Symphysodon aequifasciata* and its subspecies. Discus require very special conditions and may be considered beyond the scope of this work.

Auratus

This rock-dwelling species, *Melanochromis auratus*, from Lake Malawi, is well suited to hard water, as are most African lake cichlids. Growing to around 13cm, both fish are bright yellow with black, white-edged stripes, but at breeding time the male changes his yellow into dark blue. The female incubates fertilised eggs in her mouth until hatching occurs. The aquarium for these should have plenty of rocky caves, as they are very territorial, and plenty of green vegetable matter included for their diet.

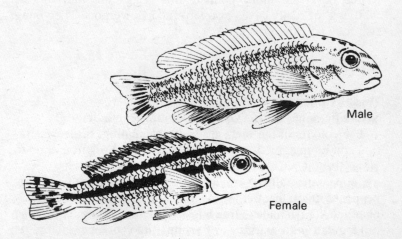

Male

Female

Fig. 27 Auratus

Lyretail Lamprologus

This fish, *Neolamprologus brichardi*, comes from another African lake, Lake Tanganyika. The light brown body helps to show off the pale blue edges to the flowing fins; the eye is also bright blue and there is a gold patch on black gill covers.

Fig. 28 Lyretail Lamprologus

Males have the more pointed fins. Eggs are laid on the 'ceilings' of rocky caves or overturned flowerpots. The young fish may be slow growers.

ANABANTOIDS

Dwarf Gourami

Scientific name *Colisa lalia*. Maximum length 5cm.

The colours of the male are truly fascinating; if the illustration can be imagined to have a delicate blue background on to which bright red markings have been thickly woven to give the appearance almost of red stripes with dozens of red dots peppered over the tail, some idea of its delicate beauty is obtained. The female is much less attractive, being more of an olive green with markings of an indefinite orange. Naturally, at breeding condition, the colours of both fish are intensified. The male feelers have more colour in them at all times.

Definitely on the shy side, the Dwarf Gourami needs plenty of plants and hiding places. It does not flourish in deep water; it likes high temperatures round 26–27°C, water that is old, but very slightly acid and soft, and some sunlight. Very fond of greenery it is almost a vegetarian and should always have some algae; it will take normal foods which are not too large for its small mouth. It is somewhat prone to catch the disease

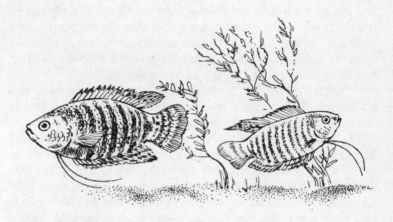

Fig. 29 Dwarf Gourami

known as dropsy if crowded and without protective clefts in the rocks that it can shelter in.

As a labyrinth breather (see page 51), it conforms to the habits of its cousins, the Lace Gourami and the Siamese Fighting Fish, with two slight differences: the breeding temperature should be 27–28°C and *Myriophyllum* should be present to be incorporated in the bubble nest. Sometimes the female helps in the construction. The nest is about 8cm across, the eggs hatching in 36 hours at 27–29°C. A tight-fitting cover is essential to help keep off draughts and dust particles for at least the first two months. They need free air to gulp as soon as they develop.

Lace Gourami
Scientific name *Trichogaster leeri*. Maximum length 10cm.

The great popularity of this fish has given it a variety of names: Lace Gourami, Pearl Gourami, Leeri Gourami or Mosaic Gourami. Its appearance is beautiful rather than flamboyant, richer in markings than in hues; with a fine pearly lace-work on the silver background, threaded throughout by an irregular black line from the mouth to the tail, this lovely fish has bold outstanding finnage and magnificent feelers.

With a wide temperature tolerance it flourishes at 23–25°C, and has a preference for old water. A small eater, it should be fed fairly often, say, three times a day. Has the virtue of eating *Hydra* when it is hungry. At least one good thicket of plants to serve as hiding place is essential, as it is not a boisterous fish and likes to retire for privacy and peace.

A labyrinth breather, it builds bubble nests in common with all its type. This peculiar breeding process is fully described in the section on Siamese Fighting Fish.

The Lace Gourami simply will not breed if it does not like its surroundings. Old, neutral water (pH 7.0) temperature of 27°C, a fairly large tank (say 60cm by 30cm by 20cm high) with some mulm at the bottom and plenty of plants, especially *Cryptocorynes*, Amazon Swords, *Aponogeton* and *Vallisneria* and also some floating plants – all these combined should induce it to spawn.

Fig. 30 Lace Gourami

The male is not as rough with the female as some other labyrinth breathers, but she should be removed after the eggs are laid; he can be left with the nest, and even with the fry for three to four days if desired.

Some 250 eggs are laid in a bubble nest measuring 9cm across and 0.75–1.5cm deep, and they hatch in 24 hours at 27°C. A tight cover is essential to keep off dust and draughts until the fry are two months old.

The sex differences are apparent even outside breeding condition: the male has extended rays along the anal fin, and his dorsal fin reaches back nearly over the tail; the female's body is plumper and her dorsal fin much shorter. When breeding, the male has a bright orange breast and feelers and never quite loses these colours if in good condition.

Siamese Fighting Fish
Scientific name *Betta splendens*. Maximum length 6cm.

Perhaps the most famous of all the aquarium fish, the male can be breathtaking in his beauty – greens, blues, reds, lavenders, purples – all hues to delight. Two males fight on sight; in fact, the national sport in Siam was to match these finny stalwarts against each other, and to place heavy bets, especially where pedigree champions were involved. During

Fig. 31 Siamese Fighting Fish

the fight, which can last several hours, fins are ruthlessly ripped and even blood can be drawn.

The aquarist can safely keep one in his tank since the male disdains to attack any other fish as being an unworthy opponent. Rather, he tends to be lazy and sulky, lurking in odd corners, and displaying his beautiful colours on somewhat rare occasions. He has a wide temperature range but prefers 23–25°C. His life span is only three years.

When the fish get to 3cm in size the sexes can be identified. The females are peaceful, drab in colour, and have shorter, more rounded fins; the males are exactly the opposite in each point.

Because they fight at even this early stage, they have to be kept in separate jars. Fortunately, these jars need not be large because the Siamese fighters are labyrinth breathers and therefore have an auxiliary breathing apparatus for taking oxygen direct from the air as well as from the water by using their gills in the normal way; deprived of this, they die.

The breeding actions are also unusual. The male fish builds a floating nest constructed of air bubbles supported by odd bits of plants, twigs, etc. The bubbles are blown by the male and are slightly coated with saliva so that they do not burst too easily; the average size of the nest is some 8cm by 5cm by just over 0.5cm. The female may help in this construction, but it is more likely to be done by her larger and more powerful mate. A good breeding temperature is 26°C and the addition of floating plants and of good light is helpful.

Incidentally, the male who is ready to breed is liable to kill a female who is not. Choosing a pair, therefore, requires considerable care; this can be done, for example, by keeping them separated by a sheet of glass until they both show signs of interest, and even then allowing them to be together for only brief periods at first. At all times, too, there should be thickets of plants or other hiding places where the female can retire for rest or protection.

The nest built, the male drives the female under it, almost wraps his body around her, turns her upside down and practically squeezes the eggs out of her. During this embrace the two fish slowly sink to the bottom. The eggs are fertilised as they are laid. This breeding action may go on for as long as an hour, and two or three hundred eggs, or even more, may be carefully gathered and wrapped in a separate bubble before being put into the nest.

When the female begins to retire to her hiding-places more and more, she should be removed. It is usually safe to leave the male behind for two days to tend the fragile nest, and industriously to replace any burst bubbles.

At a temperature of 26–28°C the eggs hatch in two days. Old water is preferred.

One final word of warning. The young fry do not develop their auxiliary breathing apparatus for three to four weeks and are peculiarly susceptible to draughts or to dust on the water surface; a close-fitting top cover is therefore advisable.

KILLIFISH

Gardneri
This fish, *Aphyosemion gardneri*, is both highly coloured and relatively short-lived, like most fishes in the Killifish group. The colouration patterns may be to help camouflage it in the sunlit but dappled areas of its native Nigerian jungle streams; many colour variants of this species occur, according to the location where each is captured.

Breeding Killifish is often quite different from other fishes, as, with some species, their eggs have to be kept almost dry for several weeks before reimmersion in water triggers hatching. Most fishkeepers tend to keep Killifish as separate spe-

Fig. 32 Gardneri

cies, even though some can be kept in a community collection with other fishes.

CATFISH

Armoured Catfish

There are a number of aquarium species of these delightful fish. Peaceful and industrious, they spend their time grubbing about the floor of the aquarium eating leftovers of food, and fully earning their title of scavengers. Their rather sleepy, lazy attitude during the day should not be misunderstood, as they are largely nocturnal. In fact, they are very hard workers. At frequent intervals, they will dart up to the air surface to take in a gulp of atmospheric air, but they are not full-fledged labyrinth breathers, although they can live in quite foul waters. As young fry, they do not appear to develop this ability under four to six weeks, and are very sensitive to lack of oxygen in the aquarium or to dust on the water surface. If prevented from reaching free air, above water, they will drown.

Some of the more popular *Corydoras* are listed:

C aeneus, sometimes called the Bronze Catfish. Prefers lower temperatures than normal, e.g. 21–23°C, breeds at 22–24°C, eggs hatch in three to four days.

C arcuatus, or Arched Catfish, after the dark arching line running from eye to tail, so pronounced on its pale body.

Fig. 33 Armoured Catfish

C julii, or Leopard Catfish, from the very beautiful markings all over its body, dorsal fin, and tail. Has three horizontal stripes on each side, and a black spot on top of its dorsal fin.

C melanistius, very similar to the *julii* except that it does not have the horizontal side stripes and dorsal spot but two dark vertical smudges on the body, one through the eye and the other from the forward base of the dorsal fin.

Our illustration is of *C paleatus*, one of the most plentiful of the 'armoured catfish'. While bringing out the barbels and heavy scaling, justice has not been done to the blue/back dappled markings found on the body, especially under the dorsal fin. In common with the others, it grows to 6–8cm in length.

Breeding is easy. The female is more plump and full bodied, her dorsal and ventral fins are more rounded, and her belly and the first ray of her pectoral fins are slightly tinged with colour.

Love play starts with the male repeatedly swimming over the female, caressing her with his barbels, and ends with them locked together, the male lying on the floor heeled right over with the female resting her chest on his. On separation, the female carries the eggs in her ventral fins to the chosen plant, or aquarium glass, which she mouths thoroughly before pressing the adhesive eggs onto the surface. The spawning may last for an hour or two before parents ignore each other and the eggs. Just as a precaution, however, the adults should be removed.

The spawning tank should be 15–23cm deep, with clean gravel, some strong-leafed plants like *Sagittaria* or Amazon Sword plants, with mature water and a temperature of 23–24°C. The eggs hatch in 72–96 hours at 23°C.

Glass Catfish
Scientific name *Kryptopterus bicirrhus*. Maximum length 10cm.

One of the strangest of all aquarium fish, it is almost completely transparent, and our illustration endeavours to show that apart from the sac containing the internal organs and the bone structure, very little else is visible!

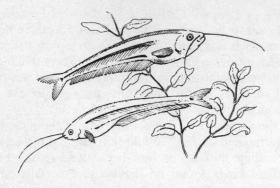

Fig. 34 Glass Catfish

With advancing age, the glass-like appearance yellows and it tends to become opaque.

A peaceful fish, it is very short-sighted and therefore has difficulty in catching such foods as live *Daphnia*. *Tubifex* worms are traced by means of its long feelers which are stretched right forward when it is on the hunt.

Prefers old water and a fair amount of mulm at the bottom of a thickly planted tank of *Cryptocorynes* and Amazon Swords.

Has a disconcerting habit of staying in one place, usually a few inches below water surface, and 'shivering' (rippling from side to side almost as though it had the disease called 'shimmies'). Temperature 25–28°C. Dislikes light. Quite hardy. Likes to shelter under broad leaves.

Sucking Catfish
Scientific name *Otocinclus affinis*. Maximum length 5cm.

Another peculiar fish, the large suction mouth is useful in holding the fish in chosen positions, or it can be used as a miniature vacuum cleaner to remove food and algae from glass sides, rocks, plants, leaves, etc. When in an upside down or vertical position, it uses its strong pectoral and ventrals to hang on.

Peaceful, hardy and very industrious, it likes well-planted tanks, old water, not too much mulm, and sunny locations to

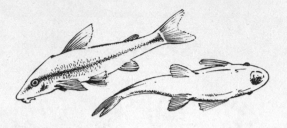

Fig. 35 Sucking Catfish

help develop algae. Temperature preferred is 24–27°C. It hates bare empty tanks with no normal foods, but is a little inclined to overfeed on *Tubifex*. Aeration welcomed.

It breeds in a similar way to *Corydoras aeneus*.

LOACHES

Kuhli Loach
Scientific name *Acanthophthalmus semicinctus*. Length under 8cm. (Other kinds grow much larger, to the detriment of the aquarium.)

In common with the *Corydoras*, these are also noted as scavengers. There are several kinds, of which one only is described here.

Our illustration shows the pale belly, the barbels, the dorsal and the pectoral fins. The ventral fins are halfway along the body length, often at the seventh set of markings counting from the tail, i.e. two markings past the dorsal.

Above water vegetation to give streaked light and twigs on the top 3cm of water is essential for breeding. The male persistently swims over the female and caresses her with his barbels. It is believed to like fairly high temperatures, 25–29°C, and to appreciate aeration. As with the *Corydoras*, it is nocturnal. It will eat most foods and is quite hardy. Likes twigs to perch on, or gaps to hide in, even when adult.

Fig. 36 Kuhli Loaches

OTHERS

Glass Fish

Scientific name *Chanda ranga*. Maximum length 4cm.

As indicated by its name, it has a glass-like transparency showing the intestines, swim bladder, backbone, and even the

Fig. 37 Glass Fish

small bones; an outside light shone through the side of the fish gives a most pleasing effect. There is a strong tendency to go yellow and opaque with age.

Normal temperature should be 23–26°C and very old or even brackish water is preferred.

Sex differences are more apparent at breeding condition with the blue rimming on the dorsal and the anal fin being stronger on the male. In our illustration, the top lefthand fish is the male, with rounded intestines; the female in the bottom lefthand corner has her intestines hollow at the top.

When conditioned to breeding stage, a change to neutral or even very slightly acid water will often stimulate the fish into action, particularly if the temperature is raised to 26–28°C.

The tank should be 13cm deep and planted with *Cabomba* and *Myriophyllum* to catch the adhesive eggs; these hatch in a day at 27–28°C. The spawning actions are spread over 2–4 days; the eggs and fry are not always eaten by the parents who should be removed as a precaution.

The fry are minute in size and finding small enough food is the main difficulty in rearing them. Infusoria made with cow dung is best. Fortunately, the babies grow very fast, especially in a large tank (say, 80cm long by 20cm high by 30cm wide), and will soon take normal foods.

Scat

Quite striking and with the approximate shape of the Discus, although the body is more oblong than round. The Scat, *Scatophagus argus*, is nicely marked (and there are several varieties) and medium priced. Likes salt and has to be acclimatised (by the dealer) to fresh water before sale. Unacclimatised specimens are offered for sale cheaply but are almost literally a dead loss!

12

TROPICAL FISH FOR THE AQUARIUM: MARINE FISHES

In years past, marine fishkeeping was a decidedly precarious affair due to many things – lack of knowledge, weakened stock due to lengthy transportation time, lack of specialist equipment and so on. Today, marine fishes can be kept with almost the same success as their freshwater counterparts as all the shortcomings have been overcome. However, that is not to say that there are no differences between marine and freshwater fishkeeping, and the would-be 'marinist' would do well to appreciate these do exist.

THE PROBLEMS WITH MARINES

1. Water Quality Maintenance
First and foremost is the ability of the marine fishkeeper to maintain optimum water conditions in the aquarium. The reason for this is simple. Saltwater fish live in an extremely stable set of water conditions and cannot readily adapt to (or tolerate) any variations from the norm, unlike freshwater species, which originate in many varying conditions of water and, consequently, can be kept quite happily in almost any conditions once acclimatised to them. With today's commercially-available 'salt mixes,' providing the correct water conditions initially is not the problem, it is maintaining them that needs constant dedication.

2. Compatibility

Despite the myriads of fish often seen in television natural history programmes, not all marine species are happy to live together, especially in the confines of the home aquarium. Many species can be quite intolerant of not only their own kind but also of fishes that may be of the same colour as themselves! Then there are the predators to contend with – they may look exotic but must be kept in their own aquarium for obvious reasons.

3. Feeding problems

Although the majority of marine fishes are adaptable enough to take to the normal diet provided in captivity, there are some species, especially the beautiful Butterflyfishes and Angelfishes, that have such a specialised feeding regime in the wild that they cannot be catered for in captivity; attempting to keep such species is not recommended and they are best left where they are best – at home on the coral reef.

4. Availability

It is true to say that a large proportion of freshwater fishes offered for sale are bred commercially and not hauled from the natural waters. Unfortunately, this cannot be said for marine fishes, which are in the main wild-caught, although some steps are being taken to remedy this. Despite international activity to prevent it, some marine fish are still being caught by dubious means (using cyanide for instance or even using dynamite to break up reefs); in consequence, such fish are considerably stressed or weakened even before they face the arduous journey to the aquatic dealers, perhaps halfway around the world.

Fortunately, there are many aquatic dealers who not only stock marine species but are well-qualified to do so and to offer genuine, constructive advice. As its popularity grows, marine fishkeeping should rightfully take its place as an established aspect of the hobby rather than an experimental area undertaken by the courageous few.

5. Corals, Dead or Alive?

To many people, the marine aquarium is not representative without coral decoration. In the past (and originally) these were the dead, often bleached, skeletons of once living hard, or stony coral organisms. As conservation considerations become more of a priority against denuding the reefs simply for decorative artefacts (and not only for the aquarium either), there has been a growing tendency for 'mini-reef' aquariums containing living corals to become the norm. Again, the great increase in knowledge and the development of water quality maintaining equipment has made this 'back to nature' progression possible.

6. Invertebrates or not?

Along with living corals, the inclusion of invertebrate life is also a feature of the marine aquarium. Shrimps, Prawns, Sea-anemones, Sea fans, and other soft corals can now complement the undersea scene in the aquarium. However, two factors should be borne in mind – predation by the fish and the problems to be faced when medication (usually lethal to invertebrate life) needs to be used.

7. Plant Life

A notable feature of the fully-furnished freshwater aquarium, aquatic plants, is sadly lacking from the marine aquarium. The only 'greenery' available for decoration is macro-algae (*Caulerpa* spp) and the cultivation of this often requires an increase in lighting levels using more powerful lamps. This increase in lighting levels will also benefit any algae growing within the cells of live corals. Whilst in freshwater aquaria, the growth of algae is usually regarded as an unwanted occurrence, in the marine aquarium it is positively beneficial as many fish graze upon it.

KEEPING THEM HAPPY

The Aquarium

Today's modern aquarium is quite suitable for keeping saltwater fishes. Its all-glass construction avoids the past problems of corrosion from sea water which plagued metal-framed aquaria of yesteryear.

A point to note when choosing the aquarium size is that stocking levels of fish are not comparable to those for freshwater species. Only about a quarter of the number of saltwater fishes can be kept in the same size of tank. Generally, an aquarium of at least 90cm in length by 38cm in depth and width should be considered an adequate starting size.

Whilst not obligatory, thought should be given to the advantage of housing the aquarium in (or above) a suitable cabinet so that the necessary filtration equipment can be housed conveniently and out of sight.

Water Matters

As previously discussed, water quality is of prime importance. Whilst its preparation is not difficult – simply add the salt mix to the necessary amount of water, test the Specific Gravity at the proposed aquarium temperature adding more salt or more water to arrive finally at the desired figure – a certain discipline to maintaining its condition has to be observed.

Regular partial water changes (using pre-mixed salt water conforming to the SG and temperature requirements) must be undertaken. Monitoring the water conditions should be undertaken during the first few months of the marine aquarium's existence until you get used to its pattern of operation. A falling pH (sometimes accompanied by a yellowing colouration) is indicative of failing water quality.

Following the physical setting up of the aquarium, once the water temperature has stabilised, it is necessary to wait until the biological filtration system has matured, i.e., that the bacterial colony has become established in order to be able to deal with any waste products from the fish once they are introduced. To discover if this has been accomplished, test the water for ammonia and nitrite during the ensuing days and weeks. At first, the ammonia levels will reach a maximum and then decline, followed by a similar rise and fall in nitrites. Once both these levels have reached, and remain, at a minimum value (usually zero) then fish may be gradually introduced. Do not introduce the theoretical maximum numbers of fish the tank should be able to hold all at once, but work up to it over a period of months; this will allow the bacteria in the filter to multiply and keep in step with the increasing amount of waste products as more fish are added.

Heating, Filtration

The heating of the marine aquarium is achieved in exactly the same way as the freshwater tropical aquarium, and needs no extra description here.

Filtration is essential and an efficient biological system is mandatory. Whereas a basic system can be fitted beneath the substrate (sub-gravel system) a remotely-situated filter can also be used. In tailor-made reef tanks, the filtration system can be built into the tank itself, being hidden behind a black panel at one end or in the corner.

As discussed in an earlier chapter (see Sub-gravel Filters, Chapter 3), the biological filter will convert nitrogenous wastes first to nitrite and then to even less toxic nitrate. A further filter system can be designed to work (almost in reverse) to convert nitrate back to nitrogen gas thus completing the purification of the aquarium water. You can now appreciate the need for an aquarium cabinet!

Water movement created by filtration systems is welcomed by marine fish and, in the more elaborately set up aquariums, extra water pumps set at different levels in the tanks can be operated by time switches to simulate tidal movements or turbulence as found in nature.

In order to remove pollutants from the water, which the normal mechanical or chemical filter will not do, a protein-skimmer should be fitted. This is a cylindrical chamber immersed vertically in the aquarium through which a vigorous air stream is passed; protein in the water is drawn into the chamber and becomes attracted to the air bubbles, and the over-flowing 'froth' is collected in a cup on the top of the unit above the water surface from where it can be regularly removed.

Often associated with the protein-skimmer (whose operation is physically isolated from the fish in the aquarium) is the use of ozone. This unstable variant of oxygen is a powerful oxidiser, and will kill off many parasites that come into contact with it. It virtually acts as a steriliser but must be used with caution as any excess ozone produced which escapes from the aquarium can cause nausea to the fishkeeper. Ozone is produced by a unit in which air (fed from the aquarium air-pump) is subjected to a high voltage electrical discharge

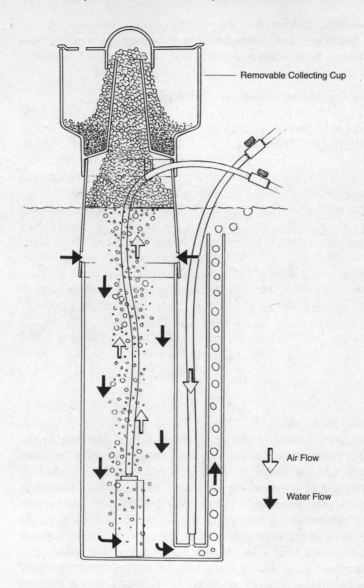

Removable Collecting Cup

Air Flow

Water Flow

Fig. 38 Protein-skimmer
(lent by kind permission of Coral Bazaar Aquatic Centre,
Walton-on-the-Hill, Surrey, telephone 01737 812475)

before being delivered to the protein-skimmer chamber. In this way fishes are kept separated from the ozone gas which would otherwise 'burn' their gills.

Decor (corals, macro-algae, lighting)

Rocks and coral heads are necessary in the aquarium to give the fish some feeling of security and places to shelter as they would find in nature. These static decorations are, of course, 'dead' materials which should be thoroughly cleansed before use. Any empty shells should be carefully examined for traces or remains of their previously living occupants and similarly cleaned.

The intensity of lighting (the 'on time' is usually twelve hours daily, although the coral reef does get its share of cloudy days and perhaps murky water) should be increased by two- or fourfold where the growth of beneficial macro-algae is required or where growing invertebrates such as soft corals is envisaged.

To achieve this intensity of lighting it may be necessary to change from fluorescent tubes to 'over-tank' hanging pendant fittings using metal halide lamps. Installing these lamps needs care: they must be situated close to the water surface to make maximum use of their light output but not too close as to suffer splashes from the water (always use a cover glass) or to affect its temperature.

Buying Fish

Apart from assessing the apparent health of the fish in the display tank, always make sure it is eating properly (you can always ask the dealer to feed it!). Ask the dealer what its regular diet consists of – to see if you will be able to sustain its needs in your aquarium. Always buy healthy, and compatible, stock, remembering that some species are best kept as single specimens in the community collection. Most marine fish are active and alert but don't be put off by some swimming with folded fins (usually a sign of ill-health in freshwater species), this is quite normal for marines; neither should you panic if some fishes appear to be lacking in some of the paired fins – for instance, triggerfishes only have rudimentary stumps where their pelvic fins should be.

Aquarium Maintenance

The upkeep of marine fish follows the same pattern as any other aquarium: the provision of optimum conditions together with correct diets for the fishes kept.

Maintenance tasks also follow the same pattern, removal of debris, decaying matter, regular water changes and the cleaning of glass panels and so on. The only real extra consideration (although it shouldn't be confined just to marine aquaria) is the attention to water conditions above all else.

SOME TYPICAL MARINE FISHES

Acknowledging that, in general, most people are impatient when it comes to hobbies and any new interest, it is not surprising that fish are often introduced into the newly set-up aquarium ahead of the ideal time. Fortunately, there are a number of species that can tolerate this lack of consideration on the fishkeeper's part without succumbing to the rigours of the new tank. These species are often referred to as being 'nitrite tolerant.' A number of suitable species for the new aquarium (and even the new marine fishkeeper) are listed below. Bear in mind that the more 'exotic' a fish is, the likelihood is that, as well as being ever more expensive to buy, it may also have specialised feeding needs beyond your (or anybody else's) capability. Always check out your fish's requirements before buying.

In the following descriptions, the stating of any species' geographic origins (if provided) is for general interest only; where a freshwater species' origin may have a great bearing upon the water conditions it needs, all marine species require approximately the same and differentiations between needs are not relevant. A basic cross-section of species is provided to give some idea of the diversity of species available; not all are compatible with each other (nor necessarily with their own kind) and choice should be ruled from the advantage of previous research before buying unwisely.

Clownfish

Long-established favourites for the marine aquarium are the hardy Clownfishes. Also known as Anemonefishes due to their

Fig. 39 Common Clownfish

natural association with Sea-anemones, Clownfishes (several species within the genus *Amphiprion* and one species in the genus *Premnas* all native to the Indo-Pacific and Red Sea regions) swim with almost a waddling action which presumably contributed heavily to their collective common name.

Colouration of *Amphiprion* species, especially *A ocellaris* and *A percula*, usually involves a large amount of red/orange body colour which may or may not be crossed with white bands; these two species are often confused but may be differentiated by the fact that *A percula* has black edging in between the white and orange colours. There appears to be two dorsal fins, although the two-colour body patterning may accentuate this illusion; all fins are rounded.

Species amongst the 'Skunk' Clownfish group, *A perideraion, A akallopisos*, often have a white stripe along the dorsal ridge and/or white vertical streaks down across the eye.

Tomato Clownfish, *A frenatus, A ephippium, A melanopus*, have, as their name suggests, a preponderance of reddish colour which may be marked with dark patches rather than white streaks or bands.

A prominent feature of *Premnas aculeatus*, the Tomato Clown, apart from its larger size, are the sharp spines which extend rearwards from the gill cover. This species is best kept as an established pair or as a single specimen.

Although always associated with Sea-anemones, to whose poisonous stinging tentacles they have built up immunity, not

Fig. 40 Tomato Clownfish

Fig. 41 Fire Clownfish

all Clownfish depend on the security the Sea-anemone offers them to the same degree. If in doubt (and the rest of the aquarium fish are Sea-anemone tolerant) then including a Sea-anemone seems to be a prudent measure to take, if you want to give Clownfish a good home.

Damselfish
Damselfish belong to the same family *Pomacentridae* (as do the various genera of Clownfish) but they have very different behavioural characteristics. Whilst Clownfish are happy to scurry around, and in, Sea-anemones, Damselfish are constantly around coral branches; their swimming action is also distinctive – they have a curious bobbing action as if they were suspended on invisible strings from the waves above their heads.

Fig. 42 Domino Damsel

Fig. 43 Humbug Damsel

Despite their modest size, Damselfish (from the Caribbean as well as Indo-Pacific regions) can stand up for themselves even against much bigger fishes if they have a mind to it. Generally they are brilliantly coloured and will add colour and activity to the aquarium. Like the Clownfishes, they are hardy enough to survive whatever the newcomer throws at them in respect of inexperience.

The most commonly-kept species include several of the *Dascyllus* genus: although these are not so brilliantly coloured (unless you get excited over black) as some other Damsels, they are generally easy to obtain at any time from aquatic outlets.

Dascyllus trimaculatus, the Three-spot or Domino Damsel, is a black fish with three white spots – one on each side, and one on the forehead. *D aruanus* and *D melanurus* are known as Humbug, or Black and White Damsels; their silver bodies are crossed with velvety-black stripes and their single fins (with the exception of the tail) are also black.

Many of the electric-blue Damsels not only have yellow tails but also provide a confusion of identification; this is due to their being found in many locations throughout the tropical seas of the world with each 'discovery' attracting yet another taxonomic name!

Amongst names you might come across include *Abudefduf (Paraglyphidodon) melanopus*, *A parasema* (formerly *Pomacentrus melanochir*), *A saxatilis*, *Chromis*, *Chrysiptera cyanea*, *Neoglyphidodon*, *Stegastes*. Such is the number of species and colour forms, it's probably prudent to take the attitude of 'a rose by any other name,' pick the fish you like the look of and worry about the name afterwards.

With such a diverse number of species, it is not surprising that the dietary variations range from herbivorous to omnivorous, however it is fortunate for the aquarist that they all acclimatise readily to captivity and accept most offered foods eagerly.

Since the members of these two groups of modest-sized fishes are egg-depositors (similar to freshwater cichlids) rather than egg-scatterers, they are beginning to be increasingly bred in captivity, and stocks, especially of Clownfishes, are beginning to appear in the trade.

Butterflyfish

The Butterflyfishes are, perhaps, everyone's idea of a coral reef fish (apart from Sharks, that is). Their disk-shaped bodies are thin enough for them to investigate amongst the coral heads in all tropical seas as they search for food in its many crevices. Their colouration serves at least two purposes – camouflage in the dazzling, ever-changing lighting of the coral reef and species recognition, obviously – but many have 'eye-spots' on the body to divert attention from the real eye (often hidden in a dark-coloured patch) which is a great help if another fish picks a fight with you.

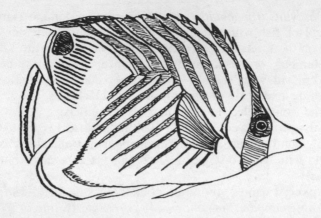

Fig. 44 Threadfin Butterflyfish

Fig. 45 Pakistani Butterflyfish

As previously mentioned, the more exotically-patterned species have extremely specific feeding requirements as in nature; for instance, they may only feed on a certain type of marine sponge whose nutritional value cannot be replicated

Fig. 46 Long-nosed Butterflyfish

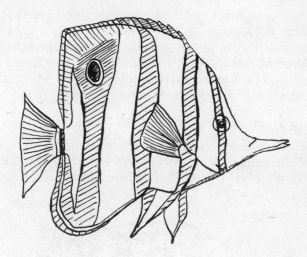

Fig. 47 Copperband Butterflyfish

commercially for the home aquarium use. Hence, the fish is doomed to a slow starvation to death if purchased by an unknowing aquarist.

Of the suitable species, the Threadfin Butterflyfish, *Chaetodon auriga*, is perhaps the oldest aquarium favourite, closely followed by *C collare*, the Red-tailed or Pakistani Butterflyfish, and *Forcipiger longirostris*, the Long-nosed Butterflyfish. The Copperband Butterflyfish, *Chelmon rostratus*, whilst very popular, has proved to be delicate and hard to keep.

Butterflyfish require plenty of swimming space and room in which they can feel they have their own territories. They are good barometers of water quality as they are amongst the first to show sign of distress if this important parameter is neglected; they usually fall victim to Marine White Spot (*Cryptocaryon*) and Velvet (*Amyloodinium*) before other species in the tank. Well-oxygenated water and a good filtration system (including a protein-skimmer) are essential to their well-being.

They can be finicky feeders especially immediately following their introduction to the aquarium (isn't it always the way?). But they can usually be encouraged to eat when offered live foods and meaty shellfish morsels (frozen or freeze dried, as well as 'raw'). Butterflyfish may munch on Sea-anemones too and can also appreciate algae-based foods.

Angelfish

Equally attractive to the marine fishkeeper are members of the Angelfish group. More robust-looking than Butterflyfish, Angelfish can be further distinguished by the presence of a

Fig. 48 Flame Angelfish

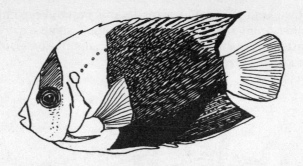

Fig. 49 Bicolor Angelfish

Fig. 50 Eibl's Angelfish

backward-pointing spine at the base of the gill cover. The size range of Angelfish reaches from around two inches to around twenty-four inches and species are found in all tropical seas, with the majority coming from the Indo-Pacific areas. Like Butterflyfishes, Angelfish too have members who are difficult to feed in captivity due to their very selective diets in the wild.

As often 'loners' in nature, until breeding forces them to be sociable for a short time, Angelfish are frequently intolerant of their own kind in captivity. Usually it is best to keep only one Angelfish from any genus per aquarium – some experienced aquarists may even limit it to one Angelfish in order to keep the peace.

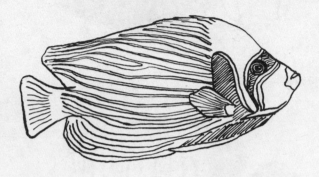

Fig. 51 Emperor Angelfish

Fig. 52 French Angelfish

Most Angelfish are by nature sponge, coral or algae grazers but can be weaned on to the usual marine aquarium meaty and algae-based foods.

A feature of the larger species of Angelfish is the colour difference between juveniles and adults. In the main, juvenile

Fig. 53 Blue-girdled Angelfish

colouration is a combination of a blue body with white markings of some description which bear no resemblance at all to the adult fish. Angelfish from the Caribbean have juvenile colouration of black with vertical yellow bands – a far cry from the often sombre black or grey colours of the 50cm long, heavily-built adults.

For the owner of a modest-sized aquarium the genus *Centropyge* contains a host of diminutive Angelfish, all of which are both well-behaved and hardy, and therefore quite suitable for a community collection of fishes.

The Flame Angelfish, *Centropyge loriculus*, has a flame-red body partially crossed with purple stripes, a yellow tail and purple edges to its flame-coloured dorsal and anal fins. The

Fig. 54 Queen Angelfish

Bicolor Angelfish, *C bicolor*, has a yellow front half of the body (apart from a blue patch on the forehead), a bright blue rear section and a yellow tail. Its fins are coloured correspondingly to whatever part of the body they adjoin. Compared to these two species, Eibl's Angelfish, *C eibli*, is a positive understatement in colouration – a grey/silver body crossed with thin gold lines; the tail is dark blue/black and the throat and pelvic fins gold-yellow.

On the larger scale, averaging around 10 inches or so upwards, such species as the Emperor Angelfish, *Pomacanthus imperator*, the French Angelfish, *P paru*, the Blue-girdled Angelfish, *Euxiphipops navarchus*, and the Queen Angelfish, *Holocanthus ciliaris*, all represent the glamour stars of the marine aquarium with outstanding colour patterns.

Gobies and Blennies
Still working on the 'small is beautiful' basis, members of the *Gobiidae* family are delightful, small, bottom-dwelling fishes that fit in perfectly into any set-up where they are not likely to be threatened by larger, boisterous (or predatory) fishes.

Cylindrical in shape, Gobies can be distinguished from Blennies by their pelvic (ventral) fins which are often fused together to form a suction disc, which anchors them in position and prevents them being washed away from their chosen position by tidal currents. Many are brilliantly coloured and some species are regularly bred in the aquarium.

The Purple Firefish, *Nemateleotris decora*, and the Firefish, *N magnifica*, are spectacularly marked with the rear portions of their bodies a rich purple and flame-colour respectively, each body being topped off by a stiffly held erect slim dorsal fin.

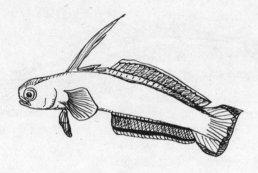

Fig. 55 Purple Firefish

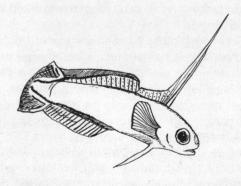

Fig. 56 Firefish

Fig. 57 Catalina Goby

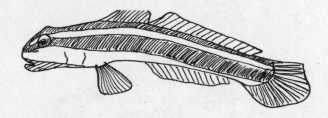

Fig. 58 Neon Goby

No less colourful is the Catalina Goby, *Lythrypnus dalli*, whose bright red/orange body is regularly crossed by brilliant-blue vertical stripes.

Living very much up to its common name, the Neon Goby, *Gobiosoma oceanops*, has an electric-blue stripe running from head to tail along the top half of the body. This Goby is well known for breeding in captivity. Sex differences are hard to evaluate and many aquarists rely on a group of neon Gobies sorting out partners for themselves and watching them spawn on almost any firm surface or in plastic pipes.

Blennies are also cylindrical in shape, have long-based continuous dorsal fins (Gobies have two separate dorsal fins) and growths resembling eyebrows called 'cirri' on the forehead. Most are active fishes, scuttling about on the substrate or

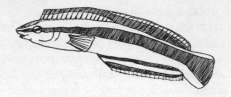

Fig. 59 Sabrefin Blenny

dashing in and out of hideaways in the rockwork.

The genera *Ecsenius* and *Meiacanthus* are very colourful but, be warned, there are other species about which are similar in appearance and which mimic the colouration of Blennies in order to approach larger fish so that they can bite chunks of flesh out of them! *Plagiotremus laudandus flavus* mimics the Forktail Blenny with this aim in mind.

However, the Blenny group must admit to having a traitor in their midst too: the Sabrefin Blenny, *Aspidontus taeniatus*, imitates the Cleaner Wrasse to achieve the same purpose but can be identified by its underslung mouth – the true Cleaner Wrasse has a mouth at the tip of its snout.

Triggerfish, Surgeons and Tangs

Apart from their obvious visual appeal, tropical marine fishes often have other interesting physical characteristics. Take Triggerfish for instance. These fish have developed a 'lockable' dorsal fin which can be fixed in the upright position to prevent the fish being swallowed or even removed from a crevice in the coral in which it has lodged itself. The locked fin then can only be folded down into its normal position in a groove on the back (in front of the usually-seen second dorsal fin) by releasing the 'trigger' mechanism. Triggerfish lack pelvic fins and many have garish patterning around the head with often the mouth accentuated to give the impression of size – another ploy to deter attacks from predators, although with their powerful jaws they should acquit themselves quite easily. They will use their jaws on invertebrates so they are not considered a good choice for a reef tank!

Surgeons take their common name from the erectile spines set on the caudal peduncle part of the body just ahead of the tail fin. These scalpel-sharp spines are normally carried flat against the side of the fish until needed in defence. Tangs (from the German word Seetang – for seaweed, which indicates their feeding regime) are tall fish with steeply-sloping

Fig. 60 Clown Triggerfish

foreheads and also carry 'scalpels.' All are herbivorous by choice and the aquarium should therefore be capable of maintaining a good growth of algae for their benefit. These fish are safe with invertebrates.

The Clown Triggerfish, *Balistoides conspicillum*, is a favourite with its bizarre colour patterning which serves to break up the traditional fish shape, again a camouflage or deterring pattern. It may be considered a delicate fish with a short aquarium life.

The black head, blue body and yellow fins make the Powder Blue Surgeon, *Acanthurus leucosternon*, an instantly recognis-

Fig. 61 Powder Blue Surgeon

Fig. 62 Regal Tang

able species but one also with a short track record as an aquarium fish.

The Regal Tang, *Paracanthurus hepatus*, is also known as the Palette Surgeon no doubt because the blue and black patterning of its oval-shaped body resembles the shape of a painter's palette, complete with thumb-hole.

The Lipstick Tang, *Naso literatus*, is also classed as a Unicornfish since many of its relatives sport a single 'horn' or protuberance from the forehead. The Lipstick Tang has immaculate 'make-up', with the mouth clearly defined. There are two orange, fixed bony plates on the caudal peduncle where Surgeonfishes' scalpels are normally situated.

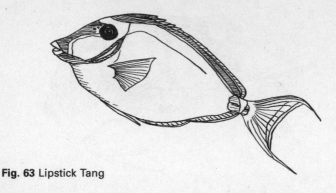

Fig. 63 Lipstick Tang

Wrasses

Would you believe some fishes put themselves to bed at night, tucked up snug in a cocoon-like wrapper? Would you also believe that the same group of fishes have members who see it their public duty to go around cleaning off parasites from other fishes? If you can answer 'yes' to both of these questions then you are already familiar with the Wrasse family.

Unfortunately, trade in collecting these Cleanerfishes from the reef leaves the other fishes at peril from increased attacks from parasites, whilst in the aquarium the Cleaner-fish can't find enough parasites to survive on. If you want to observe cleaning services in action, then one or two species of Shrimp, such as *Lysmata* or *Periclimenes*, will do just an effective job, but then you will have to ensure your aquarium is 'Shrimp safe.'

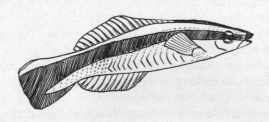

Fig. 64 Cleaner Wrasse

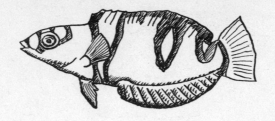

Fig. 65 Clown Wrasse

Some Wrasses, in the same way as Angelfish, have juvenile colouration far removed from that of the eventual adult.

The aquarium for Wrasses should have a substrate of a soft constituency into which they can burrow at night to rest. Apart from the specialist diets required by the Cleaner Wrasses, most Wrasses are hearty eaters and accept most 'meaty' foods eagerly. Don't be tempted to hand-feed them – they have very sharp teeth!

The Cleaner Wrasse, *Labroides dimidiatus*, is a cylindrical blue and white fish with a dark stripe running from snout to tail. Its mouth is situated at the very tip of its snout which identifies it from the voracious Sabre-fin Blenny which has an underslung mouth.

The Clown Wrasse, *Coris gaimardi*, is exceptionally coloured when juvenile – an orange body with black-edged white areas; when adult (at around 15 inches!), its colours change to green and blue on the body, a yellow tail, red dorsal and anal fins and green streaks on its face.

Seahorses

Who could resist these quaint creatures as an aquarium subject? The answer should be 'everyone' for they present quite a few problems for the marine fishkeeper. It's the usual problem – feeding.

Seahorses have tiny, tube-like mouths and need to consume copious amounts of food each day; unfortunately they prefer their food to be live, as well as abundant, and it's the problem

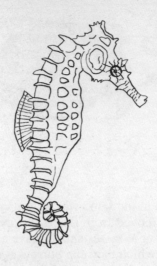

Fig. 66 Seahorse

in providing this specialised food supply that usually con-
demns the aquarium Seahorse, *Hippocampus spp*, to a slow
starvation.

Having said that, the rewards for overcoming this feeding
challenge would be enormous. Their life-style is extraordinary
with the female depositing her eggs into the male's abdominal
pouch to hatch thus rendering the male well and truly pregnant! Pregnant males are often caught in the wild and their
offspring raised in public aquaria for eventual re-release into
the wild, but the captive breeding of Seahorses is not a
common occurrence. Add to this, the demand for Seahorses
for traditional oriental medicines and you can see that this
species is truly endangered. On balance, this fish is not
recommended for the aquarium.

13

YOU AND THE HOBBY

Where else can you get a pet that is tame; that learns to know you personally; that will come when you call; that will so easily spawn for you and present you with extra pets, newly born; that will let you go away all day or even for days on end without bothering about feeding, without wondering if it will make a noise, without worrying if it will cause a mess, without needing to be taken out for exercise, or even to be given attention at any particular fixed times; a pet that has such lively colours and shapes; that looks so attractive in its miniature water garden; that intrigues and delights your guests; that furnishes a gently soothing and absorbingly relaxing point of interest; a pet that will do all that and yet need only five minutes' attention *per week*.

The fact that your pets need so little attention does not mean that they can get along without any at all! So please do be considerate. If things go wrong, it may be the fault of the dealer, it may be the fault of the fish, or it may be your own.

The dealer should do his very best to provide only healthy fish, but how can he possibly *guarantee* that a living thing will not fall sick? After all, you take great care of yourself, provide yourself with the best practicable living conditions and food, but could *you* guarantee that you would never fall ill or need a doctor?

In the vast majority of cases the customer-dealer relationship is a very harmonious and close one, but there is the exception (fortunately very rare) of the selfish customer who always demands that his work be done now, oblivious of what others may need, and who blindly assumes that the dealer has nothing else to do but to serve him. In his own eyes, too, this customer can do no wrong; if there is a fault, then it must be someone else's – never his.

The aquarium is very simple to keep, is very beautiful and does not need a lot of attention. If yours goes wrong, then there is a reason and that reason can be found and eliminated if you work with your specialist dealer.

In passing, you might like to know that over 480 varieties of tropical fish are currently sold in the better specialist shops; all these fish being peaceable, with a good temperature and food tolerance. It is naturally not possible to list all in this book, so you can well afford to experiment with new fish – on the advice of your dealer.

In addition to a good customer-dealer relationship, there is another excellent avenue open to you wherein you can take advantage of specialised (and helpful) knowledge, experience a good social scene and benefit from an ever-expanding source of aquatic information: the local aquarium society (perhaps around 400 in the UK). This will have amongst its members people who have experienced, and conquered, all the small problems that you may come across. As they are in your area, it follows that water conditions and local fish availability are all known to them. Who better to turn to for really on-the-spot practical advice? The address of your nearest society can be found through the monthly hobby magazine, the local library, or from the Federation of British Aquatic Societies.

INDEX

RIGHT WAY
PUBLISHING POLICY

HOW WE SELECT TITLES
RIGHT WAY consider carefully every deserving manuscript. Where an author is an authority on his subject but an inexperienced writer, we provide first-class editorial help. The standards we set make sure that every **RIGHT WAY** book is practical, easy to understand, concise, informative and delightful to read. Our specialist artists are skilled at creating simple illustrations which augment the text wherever necessary.

CONSISTENT QUALITY
At every reprint our books are updated where appropriate, giving our authors the opportunity to include new information.

FAST DELIVERY
We sell **RIGHT WAY** books to the best bookshops throughout the world. It may be that your bookseller has run out of stock of a particular title. If so, he can order more from us at any time – we have a fine reputation for "same day" despatch, and we supply any order, however small (even a single copy), to any bookseller who has an account with us. We prefer you to buy from your bookseller, as this reminds him of the strong underlying public demand for **RIGHT WAY** books. Readers who live in remote places, or who are house-bound, or whose local bookseller is unco-operative, can order direct from us by post.

FREE
If you would like an up-to-date list of all **RIGHT WAY** titles currently available, please send a stamped self-addressed envelope to ELLIOT RIGHT WAY BOOKS, BRIGHTON RD.,
LOWER KINGSWOOD, TADWORTH, SURREY, KT20 6TD, U.K. or visit our website at www.right-way.co.uk